'Written with drive and flair, this book intends to shake up criminology. It encourages it to move away from parochial concerns and towards addressing the global issues of our time. *Crimes of Globalization* is a wake-up call – for social science in general and for criminology in particular.'

Dr Francis Pakes, *University of Portsmouth, UK*

'A lucid – and provocative – introduction to the crimes of global financial institutions.'

David Nelken, *Distinguished Professor of Sociology,*
University of Macerata, Italy

'Criminology has a critical role in exposing, interpreting, explaining and responding to harms perpetrated by international financial institutions. This book provides a stimulating, controversial and provocative foundation for addressing the present injustices associated with, and future uncertainties created by, the crimes of globalisation. Not to be missed.'

Professor Rob White, *University of Tasmania, Australia*

'This compelling narrative of globalization and crime navigates the boundary between global harms and crimes and the space between the powerful international institutions of globalization and its powerless victims. Dawn L. Rothe and David O. Friedrichs, both renowned for path-breaking work in the area of global, state and white collar crime, open up new perspectives and provide fresh insights into the world of crimes of globalization. With thought-provoking case studies, conceptual clarity and theoretical imagination this book is a must-read for every truly global criminologist – teachers and students alike.'

Susanne Karstedt, *Professor of Criminology,*
University of Leeds, UK

CRIMES OF GLOBALIZATION

This book addresses immensely consequential crimes in the world today that, to date, have been almost wholly neglected by students of crime and criminal justice: crimes of globalization. This term refers to the hugely harmful consequences of the policies and practices of international financial institutions—principally in the global South. A case is made for characterizing these policies and practices specifically as crime. Although there is now a substantial criminological literature on transnational crimes, crimes of states, and state-corporate crimes, crimes of globalization intersect with, but are not synonymous with, these crimes.

Identifying specific reasons why students of crime and criminal justice should have an interest in this topic, this text also identifies underlying assumptions, defines key terms, and situates crimes of globalization within the criminological enterprise. The authors also define crimes of globalization and review the literature to date on the topic; review the current forms of crimes of globalization; outline an integrated theory of crimes of globalization; and identify the challenges of controlling the international financial institutions that perpetrate crimes of globalization, including the role of an emerging global justice movement.

The authors of this book have published widely on white collar crime, crimes of states, state-corporate crime, and related topics. This book will be essential reading for academics and students of crime and criminal justice who, the authors argue, need to attend to emerging forms of crime that arise specifically out of the conditions of globalization in our increasingly globalized, rapidly changing world.

Dawn L. Rothe is an Associate Professor of Criminology at Old Dominion University.

David O. Friedrichs is Distinguished Professor of Sociology/Criminal Justice at the University of Scranton.

New directions in critical criminology

Edited by Walter S. DeKeseredy,
West Virginia University, USA

This series presents new cutting-edge critical criminological empirical, theoretical, and policy work on a broad range of social problems, including drug policy, rural crime and social control, policing and the media, ecocide, intersectionality, and the gendered nature of crime. It aims to highlight the most up-to-date authoritative essays written by new and established scholars in the field. Rather than offering a survey of the literature, each book takes a strong position on topics of major concern to those interested in seeking new ways of thinking critically about crime.

CRIMES OF GLOBALIZATION

*Dawn L. Rothe and
David O. Friedrichs*

Routledge
Taylor & Francis Group

LONDON AND NEW YORK

First published 2015
by Routledge
2 Park Square, Milton Park, Abingdon, Oxon, OX14 4RN

and by Routledge
711 Third Avenue, New York, NY 10017

Routledge is an imprint of the Taylor & Francis Group, an informa business

British Library Cataloguing in Publication Data
A catalogue record for this book is available from the British Library

Library of Congress Cataloging-in-Publication Data
Rothe, Dawn, 1961–
Crimes of globalization/Dawn L. Rothe and David O. Friedrichs.
pages cm. — (New directions in critical criminology)
1. Crime and globalization. 2. Transnational crime. I. Friedrichs,
David O. II. Title.
HV6252.R68 2014
364.16′8—dc23
2014000696

ISBN: 978-0-415-85630-0 (hbk)
ISBN: 978-0-415-85631-7 (pbk)
ISBN: 978-0-203-72740-9 (ebk)

Typeset in Bembo by
Swales & Willis Ltd, Exeter, Devon, UK

Printed and bound in Great Britain by
TJ International Ltd, Padstow, Cornwall

For our grandchildren: Danny, Breahnna, Branden, Ariana, and Indy, with our hope that they and their generation will live out their lives in a just world with a sustainable environment.

CONTENTS

ILLUSTRATIONS

Figures

Table

NOTES ON AUTHORS

Dawn L. Rothe is an Associate Professor of Criminology at Old Dominion University. She is the author or co-author of six books and over six dozen peer-reviewed articles and book chapters dealing with related topics to crimes of globalization, including state-corporate crime, state crime, and the international criminal justice system. Her articles appear in such journals as *International Criminal Review*, *Contemporary Justice*, *Criminology and Public Policy*, *Justice Quarterly*, *Crime, Law and Social Change*, and *Social Justice*, as well as in various books. She has been a Visiting Professor and/or Guest Lecturer at a number of universities in Croatia, South Africa, the United Kingdom, and Belgium. In 2008 she received the Critical Criminologists of the Year Award of the Division on Critical Criminology of the American Society of Criminology and in 2010 she was the recipient of the White Collar Crime Research Consortium Young Scholar of the Year award.

David O. Friedrichs is Distinguished Professor of Sociology/Criminal Justice at the University of Scranton. He has published several books as well as over 130 book chapters, articles, encyclopedia entries, proceedings papers, and essays on topics such as the legitimation of legal order, radical criminology, victimology, violence, narrative jurisprudence, postmodernism, and white collar crime. His articles have been published in such journals as *Criminology, Justice Quarterly, Crime & Delinquency, Criminal Justice Review, Criminology & Public Policy, Social Research, Social Problems, Qualitative Sociology, Journal of Legal Education,* and *Teaching Sociology.* He has been a Visiting Professor or Guest Lecturer at a number of colleges and universities in Europe, South Africa, Israel, and Australia, as well as in the United States. In 2005 he received the Lifetime Achievement Award of the Division on Critical Criminology of the American Society of Criminology. He served as President of the White Collar Crime Research Consortium.

ACKNOWLEDGMENTS

We thank Walter DeKeseredy, Editor of the "New Directions in Critical Criminology" series, and Tom Sutton of Routledge for encouraging us to produce this volume and for their ongoing support. We are also appreciative of the Routledge book production staff for the role they have played in bringing this book to life.

We thank our family and friends for their support, with special thanks to Jessica Friedrichs, whose experience living among Thai river indigenous fishing people in 1999–2000 provided the original impetus for the "crimes of globalization" concept. She was the co-author of the seminal article on this topic first published in 2002, and reprinted a number of times since then. Many colleagues and friends within the field have over the years inspired and encouraged us, and a number of them have co-authored related articles with one of us: Victoria Collins, Christopher Mullins, and Stephen Muzzatti.

Our respective universities have provided us with various forms of support that allow us to pursue projects such as this one: Old Dominion University, College of Arts and Letters, and the Department of Sociology and Criminal Justice. We also thank and acknowledge the work of Stephen Young, a PhD research assistant at Old Dominion University, for helping with the format and references.

For David Friedrichs, his Distinguished Professor annual research stipend has allowed him to visit libraries and acquire books and other materials that were essential to the production of this book. We are both fortunate to have supportive department colleagues.

In this book we draw upon earlier and related publications of ours, and especially: David O. Friedrichs and Jessica Friedrichs, "The World Bank and Crimes of Globalization: A Case Study," *Social Justice*, 29 (2002): 13–36; David O. Friedrichs, "Comparative Criminology and Global Criminology as Complementary Projects," pp. 163–82, in David Nelken (Ed.), *Comparative Criminal Justice and Globalization*. Surrey, England: Ashgate (2011); David O. Friedrichs and Dawn L. Rothe, "Crimes of Globalization as a Criminological Project: The Case of International Financial Institutions," pp. 45–63, in Francis Pakes (Ed.), *Globalisation and the Challenge to Criminology*, London: Routledge (2013); David O. Friedrichs and Dawn L. Rothe, "Crimes of Globalization," pp. 769–78, in Gerben Bruinsma and David Weisburd (Eds.), *Encyclopedia of Criminology and Criminal Justice*, Volume 2. New York: Springer (2013); Dawn L. Rothe and David O. Friedrichs, "Controlling Crimes of Globalisation: A Challenge for International Criminal Justice," in Willem de Lint, Marinella Marmo, and Nerida Chazal (Eds.), *Crime and Justice in International Society*. London: Routledge; Dawn L. Rothe, "Facilitating Corruption and Human Rights Violations: The Role of International Financial Institutions," *Crime, Law and Social Change* 53, 5 (2010): 457–76; and Dawn L. Rothe, "International Financial Institutions, Corruption and Human Rights," pp. 177–97, in Martine Boersma and Hans Nelen (Eds.), *Corruption and Human Rights*. Antwerp: Intersentia (2010).

This book is much focused upon what lies ahead: the future. Accordingly, it seems especially fitting to us to dedicate the book to our grandchildren who will live out their lives in that future world.

PREFACE

This short book addresses a type of crime—namely, crimes of globalization—that has been little recognized to date, but which the authors will claim is of great consequence, and will as the twenty-first century progresses assume ever greater significance. Before proceeding, however, we will address a question that may well occur to potential readers of this book who are students of crime and criminal justice: Why should we devote any time or attention to something characterized as "crimes of globalization," which the authors concede at the outset lies well outside the parameters of traditional and current mainstream understandings of crime and criminal justice? Undergraduate criminology and criminal justice students assume that topics addressed in core courses such as Introduction to Criminal Justice, Criminology, Juvenile Delinquency, Policing, Courts, Corrections, and so forth, have some direct relevance for preparing them for prospective careers as police officers, state troopers, federal enforcement agencies, probation and parole officers, court administrators, and correctional institution personnel—or as prosecutors or criminal defense lawyers, should they go on to law school. Graduate students in criminology and criminal justice programs who plan on pursuing careers as professors or researchers also assume that the courses they take and the thesis or dissertation topics they address have some direct relevance in preparing them for their future careers. But it is our core premise—especially for students who are preparing for a career in the field that will stretch over many decades, well into the second half of the twenty-first century—that they will have to adapt to a rapidly changing world. And the world of crime and criminal justice specifically is quite certain to be transformed—on many different levels—in the decades ahead. We anticipate that to be effective in criminology and criminal justice careers it will become increasingly necessary to be well versed not only in local, state, and federal crime and criminal justice-related conditions, but in the global context as well. In an increasingly interconnected, globalized world what transpires on the global level will increasingly impact crime and criminal justice within the boundaries of countries. For those whose professional work will not involve direct engagement with the type of crime addressed in this book, we argue that such types of crime are likely to be an increasingly important part of the context within which they carry out their professional work. For example, we envision that criminal justice personnel will increasingly be dealing with migrant and immigrant populations that have been affected by crimes of globalization as addressed in this book. We also anticipate that the widespread global unrest we are witnessing at the outset of the second decade of the twenty-first century— for example, the Arab Spring, the European anti-austerity demonstrations and riots, and the Occupy Wall Street movement—will provide a foundation for an increasingly interconnected, disproportionately youth-driven global uprising against a fundamentally unjust and unsustainable political economy. The international financial institutions addressed in this book—and other global institutions of high finance—have already been and will continue to be one focus of such global protest movements and uprisings. Criminologists and criminal justice professionals need to be well-informed about the conditions giving rise to such uprisings and the targets of protests if they are to participate in responses that are both effective and in tune with promoting social justice.

Although international institutions of justice are hardly new, they are now proliferating. The International Criminal Court is still in its infancy, having only been implemented at the outset of the new century. It may well be that a growing proportion of current students of criminology and criminal justice will have opportunities to work for international and global policing and regulatory entities, and being well informed about crimes of globalization should prove helpful to such individuals. Many commentators—especially in recent years—have noted the parochialism of much mainstream criminology. We would like to think that this short book makes one modest contribution to the larger project of transcending such parochialism, and that students of crime and criminal justice on all levels will derive some benefits from such endeavors. We are not deriding, wholesale, the value of mainstream criminological scholarship and research. Conventional crime, broadly defined, is real, and clearly has multiple harmful consequences, disproportionately visited upon the disadvantaged and underprivileged. The system of criminal justice, broadly defined, is a necessary enterprise for a civilized and relatively secure society. But we also claim here that mainstream criminological and criminal justice research disproportionately serves the interests of the powerful and privileged classes, and either intentionally or unintentionally contributes to the perpetuation of many forms of oppression and injustice against the powerless and the underprivileged classes. Furthermore, we would suggest that at least some types of conventional crime and the control of such crimes have been over-studied by now, with diminishing returns in terms of achieving socially useful outcomes. Crimes of globalization and its control has surely been under-studied to date, and we like to think that promotion of greater attention to such phenomena opens up whole new areas of criminological research.

If crimes of globalization have been under-studied—or with a few exceptions hardly studied at all by criminologists—this can in part be attributed to the fact that such crimes have simply not been "visible" within the existing criminological conceptual framework. It is worth noting that there is a long history within criminology of some types of crime that were originally not visible and not addressed by criminological inquiry, but subsequently became the focus of a large and growing body of criminological work: for example, crimes of abuse against women ("domestic violence"), crimes of respectable professionals and small business owners (of the "white collar" class), crimes of corporations, crimes of states, and crimes against the environment ("green crime"). One of our objectives for this book, then, is to help render visible a hitherto largely invisible type of crime, with the hope that this type of crime too will over time become the focus of a significant volume of criminological inquiry.

We can anticipate a potential form of criticism of the call for more criminological attention to crimes of globalization and its control: any such criminological scholarship is highly unlikely to have a measurable influence on those who make and implement crime-related policies. We have no illusions about the resistance of policy-makers and practitioners to engaging in any way with such scholarship, for multiple reasons, and most especially if it explicitly or implicitly is threatening to their interests and their agenda. But has mainstream criminological scholarship been constructively influential with policy-makers and practitioners? Arguably in some limited areas it has been, but often only when it is in synch with the political agenda of policy-makers and practitioners. The policies and practices that have produced "mass imprisonment" in the United States in the recent era—with many widely demonstrated catastrophic consequences, especially for disadvantaged communities—have been adopted and implemented despite being at odds with a large body of criminological research during this era. If policy-makers consult and cite criminological research, it is often in the form of "cherry-picking" it to the extent that they find it useful for their own purposes. We do not have any illusions, then, that elite policy-makers and practitioners would be likely to be influenced by a criminology of crimes of globalization, and the policy initiatives that could be derived from such a criminology. But we also like to believe that "power from below" will expand significantly in the decades ahead, and that those at the center of "up from the bottom" transformative social policies might well be influenced by a criminology of crimes of globalization. Social activist groups, rather than state agencies, might be the natural audience for scholarship emanating from such a criminology. Altogether, we like to think that it is worthwhile to produce criminological scholarship that reveals and dissects profoundly consequential social and political conditions that are demonstrably harmful, and to harbor the hope that such criminological scholarship will ultimately have constructive consequences.

Finally, and what logically follows from the preceding observations, the crimes of globalization that are addressed in this book produce especially pervasive forms of social injustice. All students of crime and criminal justice inevitably engage with issues of justice and injustice, and are hopefully drawn to the subject matter of criminology and criminal justice due in part to their concern with justice and injustice. We are favorably disposed towards the argument put forth long ago by Richard Myren (1980), in his call for "justiciology": that the study of *criminal* justice should be intertwined with the study of *civil* justice and *social* justice. Accordingly, we hope that readers of this book will conclude that we have identified a significant form of injustice that has criminal, civil, and social dimensions.

Indeed, one potent motivating factor for the authors in producing this book is our strongly held conviction that the present architecture of the political economy of the global North and Western states such as the United States, and in a broader sense a global or international political economy, is inherently unjust and unsustainable. And as one part of this, we share with many other commentators and observers a deep-seated concern with potentially catastrophic developments in the decades ahead, which in the extreme case threaten the survival of humanity. The broader threats include (but are not limited to) "overload of the ecosystem, overpopulation, unsustainable growth, species extinction, growing inequality, global injustice . . . global warming and peak oil" (Jackson 2012: xvi). At least *some* of the potential future catastrophes and threats would be rooted in criminogenic conditions currently embedded within our political economy, and the related crimes of the powerful. We believe that it is difficult to overstate the urgency of anticipating these major threats and potential catastrophes, and fostering a broad, critical mass of scholarly inquiry that identifies as exhaustively as possible criminogenic conditions most likely to bring about the realization of major threats and potential catastrophes as well as the optimal social policies and practices that might limit, contain or mitigate these threats and catastrophes. Criminologists need to be part of this endeavor, with the present book offered as just one modest contribution to this scholarly enterprise. For criminologists who share our concerns about the future, a reordering of priorities in relation to the focus of their work might be worth considering.

This introduction has been drafted in January, 2013. If we go back eighty years, to January, 1933, a new chancellor was taking office in Germany, Adolf Hitler. What were German—and American—criminologists doing at that time, and over the next decade or so? For the most part, they were focused upon conventional offenders and juvenile delinquents, with many German criminologists in particular applying a Lombrosian "born criminal" framework to their understanding of such offenders (Gibbons 1979; Wetzell 2000). What they were *not* doing—for a range of reasons—was focusing upon the Nazi regime of Adolf Hitler and its criminogenic—and criminal—nature. And of course that regime perpetrated one of history's monumental crimes, a catastrophe in particular for European Jews: the Holocaust. For that matter, other monumental crimes of the period 1930s to the 1950s—those of Stalin's Soviet Union and Mao's China—also attracted virtually no attention from criminologists. Without suggesting any direct comparisons, we think of the call for attention to crimes of globalization as part of a broader current endeavor within criminology that addresses especially large-scale crime, past, present and future.

The conditions of globalization itself are complex. Yes, there are measurable positive outcomes from expanding globalization and from some dimensions of the promotion of free markets. But the dramatic expansion of inequality across the globe—with increasingly extreme divides between the "99 percent" and the "1 percent" and the attenuated future prospects of younger generations in many countries—is quite certain to be increasingly challenged. The Arab Spring, the anti-austerity demonstrations across Europe, and the "Occupy" movement in the United States and elsewhere are simply some of the more recent manifestations of such challenges. Although specific predictions about future global developments are always highly problematic, we are strongly inclined to believe that many forces giving rise to social anger from below will coalesce and bring about fundamental transformations. We adopt this view despite having no illusions about the immense resources available to those parties wedded to and benefiting disproportionately from the present architecture of the political economy. But fundamental change during the lifetimes of student readers of this volume seems far more likely than not. This book has been produced principally during 2013. Who in 1913, one hundred years ago, foresaw the extraordinary chain of events and the many dramatic changes that occurred over the next fifty years, between 1913 and 1963? The authors themselves have been witness to and in some cases have directly experienced the equally extraordinary chain of events and many dramatic changes that occurred between 1963 and 2013. Readers of this book in the middle of the second decade of the twenty-first century will surely witness many transformative circumstances by the middle of the seventh decade of the century. It is our claim that the crimes of globalization addressed in this short book are symptomatic of fundamental defects in the present architecture of the global political economy, and it follows from this that they have been and will continue to be one focus of discontent and anger with this architecture, especially in the global South. We regard attention to crimes of globalization as well as many cognate forms of crime—for example, state-corporate crime and international crime—as one essential component of what we characterize as a prospective criminology of crimes of the powerful: that is, a criminology that addresses not only crimes of the past and the present, but also probable crimes of the future.

The following chapters each attempt to elucidate what exactly crimes of globalization are—including some of the conceptual and definitional issues—what research has been done and several examples of these types of crimes. We propose an ambitious integrated framework to help understand why these crimes occur, and will continue to occur in the decades ahead. And we offer some insight into issues related to accountability and formal responses to these forms of social harm. We close with noting the potential of a global social movement to counter the policies and programs of the international financial institutions that produce crimes of globalization.

1

CRIMES OF GLOBALIZATION AND THE CRIMINOLOGICAL ENTERPRISE

In this chapter we propose to offer some context for our claim that crimes of globalization should be more widely adopted as a criminological concern. In the interest of supporting our claim we begin with a "genealogy" of our project here, and an identification of some underlying assumptions we bring to the project. Next, we address some of the core terms and concepts that arise in relation to crimes of globalization. We then turn to a consideration of two core concepts at the center of our project: "crime" and "globalization." Finally, this chapter concludes with a discussion of the criminological enterprise, and situates "crimes of globalization" within this enterprise as it evolves early in the twenty-first century.

A cautionary note would seem to be called for here. The relevant literature on the matters addressed in this book is vast. The challenges of globalization are endlessly complex. We are profoundly conscious that we have only identified selective dimensions of the realm within which crimes of globalization occur. For all kinds of reasons, human existence becomes progressively more complicated, with an escalation of complexities of all kinds (Spier 2010). The prominent American writer E. L. Doctorow (2008) has invoked the metaphor of Moby Dick—the white whale—to represent the thesis that the new century may be too much for us to apprehend. So we proceed here with a sense of humility, with no illusion that our account of crimes of globalization can possibly be comprehensive in all respects.

The path to crimes of globalization: underlying assumptions

Our call for criminological attention to crimes of globalization has hardly emerged in a vacuum or out of whole cloth. It is a product of many different strains of criminological inquiry.

First, our project is more closely aligned with an enduring humanistic as opposed to a positivistic tradition within criminology. This humanistic tradition draws core inspiration from the humanities—philosophy, history, literature—as opposed to the natural sciences. It stresses interpretation and description over the testing of hypotheses. It relies more upon qualitative than quantitative data. It accepts the capacity of humans to create and give meaning to their world, and to act in that world, although human action is profoundly influenced by the social environment, broadly conceived. It questions the viability of claims that true objectivity is possible in the endeavor of making sense of the world, and that social observers should always assume a stance of neutrality in relation to matters of social policy. Let us be clear: we do not dispute that work carried out within the alternative, positivistic criminological tradition has value; "scientific" studies can contribute something to our understanding of crime and its control and quantitative data can be useful. We draw upon some work carried out within this tradition when it seems helpful to do so. But the overall interpretation of crimes of globalization set forth here is more closely aligned with the humanistic tradition.

Second, we identify strongly with a multi-disciplinary understanding of the criminological enterprise, as opposed to the notion that criminology can or should claim the status of a unified discipline. The fundamental issues of crime and its control, broadly conceived, are endlessly complex, and a sophisticated understanding of these issues draws upon a wide range of disciplines. Of course it has long been acknowledged—perhaps by most criminologists—that criminology usefully draws upon sociology as a core foundation, as well as such disciplines as history, political science, economics, psychology, anthropology, and for at least some criminologists, biology and neuroscience. The significance of the scholarly field of international affairs has been far less recognized. In an increasingly globalized world, the realm of scholarship generated in relation to international affairs becomes increasingly important. Accordingly, here we draw upon knowledge and insights generated by scholars aligned with a broad range of disciplines.

Third, we reject the notion of uni-causal explanations of crime or "general" theories of crime and its control. Crime and its control are far too complex for such explanations and theories. Crimes of globalization and the control of such crime can only be understood through the application of an integrated, multi-dimensional theory of crime, and we put forth the basic dimensions of such a theoretical approach as applied to crimes of globalization in Chapter 4. Some initiatives toward the development of integrated theories have been developed within mainstream criminology, and some within critical criminology. We draw principally upon the latter efforts. Some integrated theories have been applied to conventional crime, and some to white collar crime, or to crimes of states. Again, our effort is part of the latter initiatives.

Fourth, we draw principally upon a criminology of the crimes of the powerful, as opposed to the traditional focus of criminology on the crimes of the powerless. Crimes of globalization fall under the broad ambit of white collar crime (in the European literature often labeled "economic crime") rather than conventional crime. Crimes of globalization, in colloquial terms, are "suite crimes," not "street crimes." Criminology as a whole, throughout the past century and even today, privileges attention to the latter over the former. Within white collar crime scholarship, and going back at least to the pioneering work of Edwin H. Sutherland, there has been attention to individual offenders and to organizational offenders. In relation to crimes of globalization, the principal focus is upon organizational offenders, although the role of individual actors is not wholly disregarded. A criminology of white collar crime is now firmly established. We also draw upon more recently emergent criminologies of crimes of states, sometimes characterized as international criminology or supra-national criminology.

Fifth, the general framework of criminological concern has been on crime that occurs locally, then within a "state" (in the sense of the fifty states of the United States), and then within a country (or in the American context, within federal jurisdiction). In recent years we have the emergence of a transnational and global criminology, and obviously attention to "crimes of globalization" by definition is a proposed element of a rapidly evolving global criminology. We will have more to say about global criminology later in this chapter.

Sixth, through most of its history the dominant focus of criminology has been on criminal offenders. From the 1960s on, however, a revival of the original eighteenth-century "classical" school focus on the criminal justice system itself became a very large part of the criminological enterprise, although often as part of the "field" of criminal justice. And principally from the 1970s on (albeit with earlier roots) we have the emergence of more systematic attention to victims of crime, as part of victimology and a victim's rights movement. A criminology of crimes of globalization ultimately must attend not only to offenders but to entities of control and to victims. The field of criminal justice studies has overwhelmingly—in the American context, as an example—attended to local, state and federal criminal justice agencies in relation to conventional forms of crime. These entities have to date a limited and often indirect engagement with crimes of globalization. Accordingly, we must look to international and civil society entities in relation to actual or potential sources of control over the parties that perpetrate crimes of globalization.

Seventh, for the mainstream of criminology the key term "crime" has been defined in terms of violations of the criminal law within a particular local, state, or federal jurisdiction. But an alternative tradition in relation to the meaning of "crime" applies the term more broadly. Attention to "crimes of globalization," as will be evident, is aligned with the calls for broader conceptions of the meaning of crime, and for criminological attention to harms not encompassed by the criminal law. The definition of crime issue is addressed further on in this chapter.

Eighth, during the course of its history criminology has generated a large number—some would suggest a bewildering variety—of criminological perspectives and theories. It has not been uncommon to classify many of these perspectives and theories as falling under the ambit of "mainstream" criminology, whereas many others are seen as manifestations of an alternative—non-mainstream—tradition. We identify with and draw principally (although not exclusively) from this latter tradition. We address the application of different strains of critical criminology to crimes of globalization in the final section of this chapter.

Key terms in relation to crimes of globalization

The type of crime addressed here occurs within the context of a globalized world. Much about this world and the way to best characterize it is contested. Some of the key terms that are invoked in relation to crimes of globalization are used in quite different ways, and some terms are regarded as fundamentally misleading while others are regarded as pejorative or politically incorrect. It may be useful here to identify some of these terms and to acknowledge early on the contested meaning of some of them.

Both the terms *crime* and *globalization* are hugely problematic, insofar as both terms are invoked to mean many different things. Since these two terms are literally the core terms for a project focused upon "crimes of globalization" we will address each of them at some length in the next two sections of this chapter.

Crimes of globalization principally occur within the poorer countries of the world. But how are these countries best described or labeled? For a long period of time the term *Third World* has been used for such countries. This term originated in the 1950s (inspired by the three "estates" of eighteenth-century France): the United States exemplified a *First World* country; the Soviet Union (and subsequently Russia) a *Second World* country. The economically struggling countries of Africa, Asia and Latin America—with a colonial past, in most cases—were the Third World countries. Although the term continues to be quite widely invoked, some observers reject it as arbitrary in terms of which countries should be included and pejorative in relation to the link with a colonial past. Some other terms applied to the countries where crimes of globalization are concentrated include: the *global South, developing countries*—or *least developed countries* (LDC)—*non-industrial countries, non-aligned countries, debtor countries, majority countries* (in the sense that the majority of the world's population live in such countries), and *countries of the periphery* (in World System theory). Any such terms have limitations of some kind. We have chosen in this book to go principally with the global South.

Since mention has been made of the World System, which historically has been dominated by such core countries as Great Britain and the United States, we can also note that some commentators refer to a *Global Empire* and a *New International Economic Order*. While such terms are used somewhat interchangeably, in relation to our project here the second of these is perhaps the best fit.

If the countries of the global South are the developing countries those of the *West* or *global North* are variously also referred to as *rich countries, industrialized countries*, part of the *Triad*, or the *developed countries* (with the similarity of developing and developed surely generating some confusion). These "developed" countries have long aligned themselves, most formally in the recent era as part of *G6* countries that met in 1975 in the wake of the 1973 oil crisis. With the addition of Canada they became the *G7* countries and when Russia was added they became the *G8* countries (made up of, in addition to Canada and Russia: France, Germany, Italy, Japan, the United Kingdom and the United States). Russia is sometimes classified as one of the *BRICS* countries (Brazil, Russia, India, China and South Africa) that were in an earlier era classified among the developing countries but are now viewed as "newly industrialized" with such fast growing economies that the developing country classification no longer applies. The BRICS countries first met in 2006 on their common interests, with South Africa the most recent addition (in 2010) to this group. These countries are also sometimes referred to as *Newly Industrialized Countries* (NICs). However, an important cautionary note needs to be introduced in all of this. Obviously those who live in the global North include millions of powerless, poor people, illegal immigrants among them; and those who live in the global South or the BRICS countries include millions of comfortably middle-class people and some extremely wealthy people, including billionaires. Given this, one should not think of the global North and the global South in exclusively geographical terms, but more in terms of asymmetrical global distributions of power and privilege.

In 1999 a proposal surfaced for a broader forum economic affairs council in a rapidly expanding international financial system. In 2008, in response to the unfolding global financial crisis of that year, top finance ministers of nineteen wealthy nations plus the European Union first met to address common concerns. These countries collectively account for some 80 percent of the gross world product (GWP). Hence the term *G20* countries has now surfaced as a replacement economic council for the more limited G8 countries. The G20 countries in subsequent meetings have been the target of protests that their perspective and policy proposals are skewed to favor the powerful and the privileged.

The term *Western hegemony* refers to the dominance of the developed countries of the West (or global North) not only economically but politically and culturally (and in technological terms). Somewhat more narrowly, the economic dominance of the recent era—essentially, since the 1980s (with Reagan in the USA and Thatcher in Great Britain as dominant leaders)—has been largely driven by *neo-liberalism, free market fundamentalism*, or *the Washington consensus*. All three of these terms are often used interchangeably, and refer to essentially the same thing: economic policy should privilege "free" markets and private sector enterprise—or a purely capitalist economic system—over one with substantial government or public sector controls and engagement. As Margaret Thatcher famously declared, "[T]here is no alternative." But this "free" market model is alternatively characterized as a "rigged" game greatly favoring Western corporations and financial institutions—and countries of the global North more broadly—over all other constituencies.

If "neo-liberalism" has become the dominant economic orientation of the global North countries, various theorists have promoted concepts that transcend purely economic considerations to capture essential emerging dimensions of contemporary society. Manuel Castells' (2004) is associated with promoting the concept of a *network society*. By this term Castells means that we increasingly live in a world of global networks made possible by advanced communication technologies, challenging traditional hierarchies of governance. We find this term useful in relation to crimes of globalization because global networks of public, private and semi-public/private actors and entities make such crime possible. Ulrich Beck (2008) is associated with promoting the concept of *risk society*. By this term Beck means that the intensification of dangers from environmental, financial, terrorist-driven and other global threats has dramatic consequences and has transformed the way in which people think of contemporary social existence. We regard this term as useful also in relation to crimes of globalization because at their core they involve the shifting of huge risks—economic, environmental and other—on to people in the global South countries especially poorly positioned to protect themselves from such risks.

With all the attention to an increasingly globalized and inter-connected (and inter-dependent) world there is widespread recognition that states have hardly disappeared as key actors in this world, and in some accounts they are even more potent actors than at an earlier time. The term *nation-state* is sometimes applied. The principal value of the term nation-state is that it clarifies that here one is not speaking of "state" in reference to Pennsylvania, Virginia, and so on—obviously in the U.S. context a source of confusion in relation to the invocation of the term "state." However, it assumes that a nation must be a state and on the flip side, that a state must be a nation. If one considers Palestine, which is not a recognized state but a territory and, one could argue, a nation, we can appreciate the confusion from using such a term. As such, we invoke the terms state and country interchangeably. If the states of the global North (starting with the United States) are commonly regarded as strong and generally stable, at least some of the states of the global South are characterized as weak, fragile, failed or even collapsed states. To the extent that such characterizations are warranted, the question arises: to what extent should this state of affairs be attributed to internal failings and to what extent to the policies and practices of the powerful states and the international organizations based in these states?

If the state is the premier public sector entity, the corporation is the premier private sector entity. It has long been recognized that *trans-national corporations* or *multinational corporations* are especially potent actors in the modern world. The terms transnational and multinational corporation are often used interchangeably, and abbreviated as TNCs and MNCs. The term *global corporation* has also been used for these corporations, which are typically based in the United States or some other wealthy country but have operations in many different countries across the world. There is a substantial literature by now documenting the vast range of harms perpetrated by these multinational corporations in developing countries. Although this harm parallels and sometimes intersects with the harms addressed in this book, such harm is not the focus of the present book.

The World Bank and the International Monetary Fund—a core focus in this book—are referred to as *international organizations, Bretton Woods institutions* (in deference to the locale where they were established), and *international financial institutions*. We have chosen to go with the last of these terms. The World Bank has more recently been aligned with several other international financial institutions as part of the World Bank Group. But as the World Bank itself is the highest profile of these institutions, and remains the most dominant of them, we will in the interest of minimizing confusion use the term World Bank instead of World Bank Group. The World Trade Organization (WTO) is a hugely important international organization that evolved out of the General Agreement on Tariffs and Trade (GATT). It differs from the World Bank and the International Monetary Fund insofar as its primary function is regulatory with regard to transnational trade. In the endlessly complex globalized world of the twenty-first century there are other entities that play important roles in the financing of projects in developing countries, including private bank groups such as the London Club and the Paris Club. We acknowledge their significance in this realm, but do not propose to focus on their activities in this book.

If the International Monetary Fund and the World Bank are our core focus, we also need to acknowledge the existence of a range of other international institutions and international organizations whose policies and practices impact in various ways on global economic (and political) developments, and on the well-being of the global South countries in particular. These international institutions and organizations include the United Nations (and its different units), the Organization for Economic Cooperation and Development (OECD), and the Organization of

Petroleum-Exporting Countries (OPEC). Our central focus in this book, however, is on the international financial institutions.

The policies and practices of the international financial institutions in the global South countries are largely justified in terms of promoting *development* and *growth*. Both terms are quite widely invoked as though it is manifestly obvious that development and growth are positive phenomena and forces of good in the world. But all too often development and growth are promoted in a profoundly skewed way, so that the interests of wealthy countries, benefits for the multinational corporations and well-connected global South businessmen/women, and for corrupt politicians are privileged over clear, long-term benefits for the people of these countries. Accordingly, 'development' is a concept that is contested, theoretically and politically, and is ambiguous at best. We take a more postmodern perspective and suggest that development is not an objective 'thing'; rather it is a value-laden discourse that shapes and frames the reality of power relations and global economic positions. As we hope to highlight in this volume, the global discourse of 'development' has taken on a meaning that is grounded in neo-liberal market ideologies.

The term *sustainable development* is far more in accord with development policies and practices that have long-term benefits for present and future citizens of such countries. The Human Development Rating (HDR) is an instrument used by the United States to measure a country's degree of development (based upon per capita income, educational level and life expectancy), but any such estimation is necessarily selective and limited.

On the one hand, global South countries are the recipients of a huge amount of *aid* from global North countries. Aid is generally viewed as a benevolent form of charity on the part of wealthy states. But such aid is typically extended with political strategic objectives of the wealthy countries as a primary objective. And a sustained critique of the notion that aid benefits global South countries has arisen from diverse ideological vantage points. On the other hand, when there is the expectation (or demand) that economic assistance will be repaid, we are speaking of *debt*. We will be discussing the role of international financial institutions in fostering the taking on of debt by developing countries, and the hugely harmful consequences for the citizens of such countries of this debt in a later chapter. Some critics of the policies and practices that have been complicit in imposing huge debt burdens on developing countries refer to such debt as *odious*—harmful and indefensible—debt. In particular, we will be addressing the *structural adjustment policies* (SAPs) of the international financial institutions: hugely harmful policies for the people of the global South countries that are imposed on such countries to insure that the international financial institutions, private banks, and other parties based in the global North are repaid for the loans they have made. *Debt service* obligations are crippling burdens for citizens of the global South countries. The Highly Indebted Poor Countries (HIPC) Initiative was supposed to help relieve debt burdens for over-indebted countries (Toussaint and Millet 2010). But in fact it has been interpreted as reinforcing the logic of structural adjustment, and has largely failed in its stated aim of helping the target countries.

The expanded recognition of *human rights* is one of the defining attributes of the contemporary era, especially since the proclamation of the Universal Declaration of Human Rights in 1948. There is now a vast literature—and global discourse—on human rights. The term itself is contested. On the idealistic level, human rights are basic entitlements that should be extended to all human beings, regardless of where they live. In an alternative view, "human rights" is a Western construct reflecting Western traditions and values, but not necessarily respectful of different cultural traditions in other parts of the world. Human rights concerns intersect with crimes of globalization insofar as one important dimension of such crimes involves the egregious violation of basic human rights.

The concepts of *legitimacy* and *legitimation* are hugely consequential in our world today. The essence of legitimacy is this: do people regard the system of authority under which they live as valid and deserving of compliance? When a critical mass of a country's population no longer regard the political system as legitimate you have a *legitimacy crisis*, and the very survival of the existing political system is threatened. There is a long history of political systems being brought down as a consequence, and in the more recent era the collapse of the Soviet Union as well as the collapse of regimes across the Arab world—following the "Arab Spring" uprisings—are illustrative of this phenomenon. It is our claim that crimes of globalization can contribute significantly to legitimacy crises in countries within which they occur. More broadly, going forward, they may well contribute to a global legitimacy crisis wherein the people of the global South countries rise up against an illegitimate global governance regime dominated by the power elite of the global North.

We will also be addressing in this book institutions or organizations that challenge or seek to control crimes of globalization. On the one hand, there is the formal, global system of international justice. While not a singular system, it is composed of a multitude of treaties, resolutions and entities such as the International Criminal Court. In an increasingly interconnected, globalized world the need for coordinated *global governance* becomes ever more evident (Darian-Smith 2013; Samar 2011; Zumbasen 2012). It has been suggested that this is all part of an inevitable historical progression in human history from tribal and local governance, to state, to country, to regional (e.g., the European Union), to global. But the notion of global governance has been criticized as it would centralize yet another global system of authority and power that may well result in expanded forms of corruption, oppression, and human rights violations. However, global governance in some form has been long proposed, and since the end of World War II and especially the end of the Cold War the need for such governance became increasingly evident. It exists in the sense of the range of political networks, institutions and agencies that cooperatively and collectively address global issues. The international financial institutions have been key players in global governance since their establishment. The existing forms of global governance can be regarded as more often than not enabling crimes of globalization rather than preventing or punishing them. Altogether, the countries of the West and global North and the corporations and financiers based in these states dominate global governance. The reality is that global power asymmetries work against the hundreds of millions of disadvantaged people of the global South. During the course of the twenty-first century it is quite certain that calls for a *world government* will grow. Any such government could be a hugely coercive and powerful enforcer of the interests of the rich and powerful. Ideally, it could take the form of a global parliament that advances and protects the rights and interests of all, and promotes authentic democracy. But how the global governance and world government issues play out as the twenty-first century progresses will importantly determine as well whether or not crimes of globalization are effectively addressed.

For many observers the only true potential counter to the closely aligned interests of the state, international financial institutions, and transnational corporations and banks resides with *civil society*. This concept is somewhat ambiguous and vague, but basically refers to those institutions, organizations and networks that on the one hand are not part of the state or the corporate world, and on the other hand exist outside of family and small-scale social groups (Alexander 2006; Anheier *et al.* 2012; Garton 2009). In recent years the notion of civil society has been extended to *global civil society* (Baber 2008; Kaldor *et al.* 2012). Ideally, an active global civil society promotes the worldwide embrace of human rights and humanitarian initiatives, and broad-based justice for all. *Non-governmental organizations* (commonly referred to as NGOs) are key dimensions of civil society and a global civil society and also need to be taken into account in any consideration of crimes of globalization. NGOs—such as Human Rights Watch and Amnesty International— play an essential role in exposing and calling wide attention to violations of human rights, broadly defined, that occur within global South countries, sometimes by domestic entities and sometimes as a consequence of external or international entities. We draw upon some of the information they produce—for example, the annual Human Rights Watch Report—in this book. These non-governmental organizations will have to play an important role in any initiatives to mobilize people in response to the harms of crimes of globalization.

We also have as an important manifestation of global civil society the protests that have been directed at the World Bank, the International Monetary Fund, the World Trade Organization and other powerful global entities that are widely recognized as sources of huge harm to millions of people around the globe (Broad 2002; Mason 2012; Pleyers 2011). These protests have been described as part of an *anti-globalization movement*, but also as an *alter-globalization* and a *global justice movement*. We prefer this last term. Although protesters have a range of concerns and objectives, the core issue for most is less about globalization per se than about the fact that it's globalization from above, rather than globalization from below. In other words, the policies and practices for a changing, globalizing world are chosen and implemented by economic and political elites, and are not reflective of the concerns and needs of ordinary citizens and indigenous peoples, especially those in the global South countries. The *World Economic Forum* (WEF) that has met annually in the Swiss city of Davos since 1971 (with the name formally adopted in 1987), brings together economic and political elites to address global challenges. The *World Social Forum* (WSF) that first met in Porto Alegre, Brazil, in 2001, and has since met there and elsewhere, was established as an activist counter-event to the Davos meetings, and has stressed opposition to the IMF's Structural Adjustment Policies. In different respects, then, the World Economic Forum and the World Social Forum play important roles in both enabling and protesting against crimes of globalization. The "Arab Spring" that emerged in 2011 is viewed as one dramatic manifestation of collective civil society demand for such justice, although it reflects all the uncertainties and contradictions that are part of civil society initiatives.

Crimes of globalization and the challenge of defining crime

There is significant resistance among many criminologists to engaging with the definitional issues relating to crime or to specific types of crime. They complain of "tedious" and "interminable" definitional discussions, and clearly prefer to "get on with the work" of addressing specific theoretical and empirical questions that arise in relation to crime and its control, as opposed to devoting time and intellectual energy on dialogues relating to definitional and conceptual issues. Such impatience is understandable on a certain level, and the downside of becoming "imprisoned" by definitional conundrums to the point where one is hindered from addressing concrete and consequential "real world" issues needs to be acknowledged. But the premise here is that avoidance of core definitional issues has costly consequences in relation to theoretical and empirical progress. All too often we end up with criminologists talking past each other or generating a bottomless well of confusion and misunderstanding because the core concept of "crime" is not clearly defined. This all-too-familiar term is invoked to mean quite different things in different specific contexts.

It can be safely asserted that the term *crime* has had quite diverse meanings throughout the long history of its use, although some understandings of crime have been dominant and others more marginal. Certainly there is a long and enduring history of invoking the term "crime" without any attempt to define the term. For many people the meaning of the term crime is taken to be obvious, and so obvious that there is no need to define it. For many people, then, U.S. Supreme Court Associate Justice Potter Stewart's celebrated observation about pornography (and obscenity)—"I know it when I see it"—applies to crime as well (Slade 2000: p. 4). It also seems reasonable to claim that the term crime is most widely equated with conventional criminal offenses, or violations of the criminal law, that are exemplified by the FBI's "index" crimes: murder, rape, assault, robbery, burglary, auto theft, larceny, and arson. This is surely the type of crime of most concern to the American public, along with drug-related offenses and recent concerns about terrorism, and these offenses account for most of the "mass imprisonment" of the recent era (Abramsky 2007). The largest proportion of criminological scholarship addressing crime through the present era encompasses one or more of these types of crime. But it is also indisputably true that there is a long tradition critical of the limitations of a conventional conception of crime (Henry and Lanier 2001; Tifft and Sullivan 1980). Accordingly, the claim is made that much of the focus of the mainstream criminologist is seriously skewed.

A recent anthology—Mary Bosworth and Carolyn Hoyle's (2011) *What Is Criminology?*—recognizes that there are vastly different conceptions of what criminology is and ought to be, and accordingly how crime is best defined. Such criminologists as David Brown, Chris Cunneen, William Schabas, and Stephan Parmentier conceive of crime in relation to the global financial crisis, postcolonial violations of human rights, and violations of international law. It is implicitly or explicitly stated by these criminologists that a credible twenty-first-century criminology needs to focus on such crimes of the powerful, rather than retain the field's traditional, overwhelming focus on the crimes of the powerless. There is, in fact, a long-standing tradition of critique of conventional conceptions of crime that have been advanced by self-described radical or critical criminologists (e.g., see DeKeseredy and Dragiewicz 2012; Tifft and Sullivan 1980; Watts *et al.* 2008). The "humanistic" definition of crime put forth by Schwendinger and Schwendinger (1970) is quite familiar and has been widely cited. Stuart Henry and Mark Lanier (2001), in an in-depth consideration of the definition of crime, have advanced a "prism of crime" definition (see also Agnew 2011). Altogether, the radical and critical critiques of the definition of crime promote attention to the crimes of the powerful, and take a form that recognizes that the crimes of the powerful tend to be exponentially more consequential than the crimes of the powerless. For some criminologists, the term "crime" itself is inevitably so limiting and so constrained by its historical meaning that it should be abandoned in favor of "social harm" as the focus of our concern, with criminology itself being replaced by "zemiology," or the study of harm (Friedrichs and Schwartz 2007; Hillyard *et al.* 2004). The social harm initiative usefully calls for reconsideration of how we think about crime, but has some limitations as well if it abandons the concept of crime itself.

Defining white collar crime

Within "American" criminology in particular, Edwin H. Sutherland is surely the highest profile figure associated with a challenge to the conventional definition of crime. For some commentators, Sutherland is indeed the most significant criminologist of the twentieth century. His introduction of the concept of "white collar crime" is among his more important contributions. We need not here revisit in any detail Sutherland's (1945) celebrated exchange with law professor Paul Tappan (1947), who complained that Sutherland's application of the term white collar crime to a range of activities not specifically declared crimes by legislative criminal law was unwarranted. But the essence of Sutherland's response to Tappan has remained hugely influential among subsequent students of white collar crime: the inclusion of violations of civil and administrative law as well as of criminal law could justifiably be encompassed by the term "white collar crime" because the white collar "class" has too much influence over law-making generally and criminal law-making specifically. Accordingly, limiting the definition of white collar crime to actions specifically proscribed by the criminal law excludes a huge amount of obviously immensely harmful activity carried out by the white collar class. In effect, limiting oneself to the activities specifically proscribed by the criminal law in relation to white collar crime plays directly into the hands of corporations and other powerful social actors who have succeeded in preventing the "crime" label from being applied to a wide range of demonstrably harmful activities in which they engage.

For all of the credit Sutherland deserves in relation to introducing the concept of white collar crime to the field of criminology—and, more broadly, to the public discourse on crime—he can also be faulted for having contributed to the long, ongoing historical confusion on the appropriate meaning of the term white collar crime. Sutherland simply did not devote enough time to the definitional issues and accordingly invoked the term in quite different ways with quite different meanings. Many others have grappled with the definitional issue here as well. The approach of one of the authors of this book to the definitional conundrum is laid out in a 1992 article and in multiple editions of *Trusted Criminals* (Friedrichs 1992, 2010). The basic position taken is that it makes the most sense to treat the term white collar crime as a broad-based heuristic term, a term that signifies first and foremost the negative message that here one is not addressing conventional crime or street crime, but is rather invoking an umbrella term for a broad range of quite different forms of criminal activity not encompassed by those terms. And the second stage of this process calls for setting forth a typology that usefully differentiates between the major forms of white collar crime, as well as cognate, hybrid and marginal types of such crime. In several editions of *Trusted Criminals*, crimes of globalization have been treated as a newly recognized, hybrid form of white collar crime.

The criminological mainstream, with a self-identify as a scientific endeavor, is inherently biased in favor of definitions of crime that lend themselves easily to operationalization. But it has been suggested that this bias inevitably privileges attention to the conventional forms of crime that by their very nature lend themselves more readily to operationalization. If criminology as a field has produced a very large body of literature on some types of crime—e.g., homicide, rape, assault, robbery, larceny, burglary, auto theft, substance abuse related offenses, juvenile delinquency (broadly defined)—it has almost wholly neglected other types of crime. "Crimes of globalization" is one such neglected type of crime. The policies and practices of the international financial institutions that are addressed further on in this book can in fact be characterized as "crime" insofar as they cause vast, demonstrable—and avoidable—harm; they violate a range of international treaties and accords; and they are implemented by international financial institution leaders, officers and employees who either know or clearly should know that these policies and practices will have hugely harmful consequences.

Crimes of globalization and the meaning of globalization

The policies and practices of the international financial institutions such as the World Bank and the International Monetary Fund can only be understood in the context of the notion of *globalization*. The invocation of this term has become ubiquitous and the literature on globalization has expanded exponentially in the recent era, although its meaning is far from settled (Dean and Ritzer 2012; Ellwood 2010; Smith 2013). The term "globalization" has been in wide use since the early 1970s (Fiss and Hirsch 2005). In one sense, globalization is hardly a new phenomenon, if one means by it the emergence of international trade and a transnational economic order (Ellwood 2010). In one interpretation, it originates with the rapacious pursuit of precious metals in the sixteenth century by European states (Erlichman 2010). Yet globalization has become a buzzword of the transition into the era of the new century due to the widely perceived intensification of certain developments (Dean and Ritzer 2012). It is not simply an economic phenomenon, although it is most readily thought of in such terms. Globalization also has important political and cultural dimensions (Smith 2013). The phenomenal growth in the importance of transnational corporations, non-governmental organizations, intergovernmental organizations, international financial institutions, and special interest groups is one conspicuous dimension of contemporary globalization (Ellwood 2010; Saul 2005). The term "globalization" has been introduced to capture "the imperialistic ambitions of nations, corporations, organizations and the like and their desire, indeed need, to impose themselves on various geographic areas" (Dean and Ritzer 2012: p. 547). Ordinary people lose control over their economic destiny (Ellwood 2010; Saul 2005). World markets increasingly overshadow national markets, barriers to trade are reduced, and interstate tele- and cyber-transactions become the norm (Dadush and Dervis 2013; Smith 2013; Stiglitz 2006). In the broadest possible terms, globalization today refers to the dramatic compression of time and space across the globe.

We accept here the view that globalization as a phenomenon is endlessly complex, is characterized by various contradictory tendencies and ambiguities, and is best seen as a dynamic process as opposed to a static state of affairs (Dean and Ritzer 2012). The contemporary discourse on globalization is quite contentious, characterized by claims about the effects of globalization that are often directly at odds with each other (Dean and Ritzer 2012; Fiss and Hirsch 2005; Held 2005). On the one hand, certain aspects of globalization—such as increasing global communication and interaction—are surely inevitable. On the other hand, the mission and policy choices of international financial institutions, in relation to the globalized economy, are hardly preordained and are very much open to challenge. Some commentators argue that globalization has basically increased living standards in much of the world, and that countries experiencing a rise in standards of living have done so by linking up with a globalized economy (Auerswald 2012; Dadush and Dervis 2013; Kenny 2011). No one should dispute the claim that there are many "winners" in the move toward an increasingly globalized economy. However, we strongly agree with those who allege that the winners are disproportionately wealthy multinational corporations and the losers are disproportionately poor and disadvantaged peoples in developing countries (Dadush and Dervis 2013; Skidelsky 2008; Smith 2013). Globalization contributes to an overall increase in economic inequality, fostering impoverishment and unemployment for many (Dadush and Dervis 2013; Saul 2005; Stiglitz 2006). It has been characterized as a new form of the ancient practice of colonization (Ellwood 2010). The exploitation of people in poor countries for the enrichment of wealthy capitalist institutions is a core dimension of globalization. Altogether, globalization is affecting human society in many different ways.

What is one to make of the many contradictory interpretations of globalization? Basically, today's world is endlessly complex, with many contradictory tendencies. There are ongoing tensions between the global and the local, and between globalized entities and nation-states. One should avoid sweeping generalizations about globalization. Thomas Friedman's (2005) *The World Is Flat* was a bestseller some years ago. But for every "flattening" tendency in the world today, there are countervailing bumpy, round, asymmetric and curvilinear dimensions (Ghemawat 2007; Kurlantzick 2008; Madrick 2013). For students of crime and justice—and for citizens of a globalizing world—there is much at stake in understanding, monitoring and responding effectively to developments in an endlessly complex, ever-changing world. There is no completely "neutral" method for evaluating the effects of globalization. Furthermore, there are many different possible scenarios, going forward, on how the forces of globalization will play out. Surely there will be some complex mix of positive and negative developments.

Globalization has many dimensions, then, but the following are most pertinent to the thesis of this book:

1. The growing global dominance and reach of neo-liberalism and a free market capitalist system that disproportionately benefits wealthy and powerful organizations and individuals;
2. The increasing vulnerability of indigenous people with a traditional way of life to the forces of globalized capitalism;
3. The growing influence and impact of international financial institutions (such as the World Bank), and the relative decline of power of local or state-based institutions; and
4. The nondemocratic operation of international financial institutions, taking the form of globalization from above instead of globalization from below.

A globalized criminological framework and crimes of globalization

It is possible that global developments have modified crime problems intrinsically so deeply that the earlier criminology has lost (part of) its relevance. Capitalist globalization, mass consumption, migration and attempts to keep them under control, internet, the penetration of world conflict in daily life through (threats of) terrorism, all these and other phenomena go far beyond the scope of earlier criminology.

(Lode Walgrave 2011: p. 23)

With its emergence as a recognizable field of scholarly inquiry in the latter part of the nineteenth century, the core focus of early criminological work was on understanding individual criminality. The work of the Italian physician Cesare Lombroso, associated with the notion of the "born criminal," exemplified this orientation, and even earlier the focus upon "moral insanity" as a basic of criminality (Rafter 2004a,b). A focus on "criminal minds" and biogenetic dimensions of criminality is hardly extinct early in the twenty-first century, and there is even some revived interest in it (Fischman 2011; Monaghan 2009; Raine 2013). In the early part of the twentieth-century criminologists—especially of the influential Chicago school of the 1920s—became interested in criminal gangs and groups, and the neighborhood context of crime (Gibbons 1979). Sutherland (1940, 1949), in his famous 1939 American Sociological Society presidential address and his *White Collar Crime* book published ten years later, draws attention to corporations—or large-scale organizations—operating in a national context, as significant criminal enterprises. Almost half a century later, in 1988, in his American Society of Criminology presidential address, William Chambliss (1989) highlights the significance of state-organized crime—crime emanating out of the state itself—occurring both nationally and internationally. And in the most recent era, exemplified by Katja Franko Aas's (2007) *Globalization and Crime*, as well as by a number of subsequent anthologies—e.g., Nick Larsen and Russell Smandych's (2008) *Global Criminology and Criminal Justice*, David Nelken's (2011) *Comparative Criminal Justice and Globalization*, Francis Pakes' (2013) *Globalisation and the Challenge to Criminology*, Susanne Karstedt and David Nelken's (2013) *Crime and Globalization*, and Katja Franko Aas's (2014) *Crime and Globalization*—as well as many other recent books, there is a recognition of the significance of expanding globalization and global criminal networks as increasingly significant dimensions of the problem of crime and its control.

Neither the recognition of global crime nor calls for a globalized criminology are entirely new. Paul Knepper (2012) argues that during the 1920s and 1930s the League of Nations conducted the first social-scientific study of global crime, namely the worldwide traffic of women. Then, as now, global crime threats turned out to be difficult to measure. But in our lexicon worldwide trafficking of women is better classified as transnational crime than as globalized crime: that is, essentially new forms of crime specifically made possible by the conditions of globalization. As for calls for a global or "world" criminology, they can be traced back at least to the 1970s (Larsen and Smandych 2008). However, by any measure this call has intensified and expanded greatly with the transition into a new century. Some of these calls are concerned principally with the impact of globalization on conventional forms of crime (e.g., Findlay 1999; Friman 2009), others on the increasing emergence of international institutions of criminal justice in a globalized world (e.g., Findlay and Henham 2005). This is one significant dimension of the interconnection between globalization and crime (and its control), but there are many other interconnections. Katya Franko Aas (2007), in *Globalization and Crime*, produced a pioneering survey of the range of such interconnections, and she here provides a broad framework for more focused inquiries. In effect, globalization increasingly becomes a "structuring context" for criminology (Coleman *et al.* 2009: p. 10). But it has also been correctly noted that "If globalization is a relatively recent phenomenon, it is one that has still not been subjected to any serious critical analysis within criminology" (Coleman *et al.* 2009: p. 10). As Coleman *et al.* (2009: p. 11) further observe, "What is missing in criminology is any interrogation of the contested nature of globalization itself or any consideration of what different understandings of globalization might mean for different nation states." We certainly agree that the complex, relative distribution of power between the local, the state, and the global has to be more fully explored. But in a parallel vein in relation to all of this, we have a broadening recognition of criminal harm as impacting on individuals, on groups, on neighborhoods and communities, on states, and on a global environment. The scheme outlined above may have a somewhat artificial character, but nevertheless it seems to us to capture the evolution of criminological inquiry, and the increasing calls for transcending criminological parochialism.

Criminology has been a predominantly Western enterprise. Stanley Cohen (1988), in *Against Criminology*, was among those who recognized the limitations of such a criminological orientation. Katja Franko Aas (2012) has addressed the long-standing tendency of Western criminology to produce propositions out of observations made in Western societies and apply them universally. More narrowly, criminology is disproportionately shaped by United States realities. She notes that some commentators call for incorporation of "subaltern" voices (i.e., the voices of the poor and powerless of the global South) into our understanding of developments in a globalizing world (Aas 2012). The wholesale neglect of colonialism (and imperialism) by criminologists is one consequence of this Western ethnocentrism. Maureen Cain (2000) has suggested that Western criminology is guilty of a double sin: of either romanticizing non-Western societies or of assuming that they are no different from the West. Biko Agozino (2010), in his call for a counter-colonial or post-colonial criminology, has argued that criminologists have not made a serious attempt to understand the African reality, and have in fact been complicit in the Western project of exploiting and controlling people of developing countries. This claim is not entirely new. Piers Beirne (1983), in the early 1980s, criticized "the too common practice of American criminologists going abroad and selling their crime control 'expertise' to the governments of Third World developing countries, many of which were led by undemocratic military, or, at least, U.S. Central Intelligence Agency compliant political regimes" (Larsen and Smandych 2008: p. 6). For Biko Agozino (2010) imperialism is the basic form of all criminality. Crimes of globalization can certainly be regarded as a contemporary manifestation of a long history of imperialistic exploitation of developing countries by powerful forces based in developed countries.

We do not imagine that we ourselves are free of Western (Northern) biases. Ideally, going forward, a growing number of criminologists in developing countries will address the crimes of globalization from their own vantage point, with their own framework, terminology, insights and experiences. We do not accept the claim that criminology is intrinsically aligned with Western colonialism, imperialism and oppression, or is necessarily a "control freak discipline," as Biko Agozino (2010) has characterized it. The whole tradition of radical and critical criminology has long challenged any such agenda within criminology. There are also strains of criminological inquiry not specifically associated with critical criminology—e.g., reflexive criminology, socially responsible criminology, republican criminology—that call for criminologists to be fully conscious of their own biases, to be fully mindful of possible harmful consequences of their work, and to be oriented toward the broad project of reducing inequality in the world (Braithwaite 2011; Nelken 1994; Parmentier *et al.* 2011). The term a "sparking criminology" has been applied to "transformative projects across disciplines" (Parmentier *et al.* (2011: p. 5). We hope that a criminology of crimes of globalization can "spark" cross-disciplinary, transformative projects. We like to think that a criminology of crimes of globalization challenges rather than enables imperialistic and oppressive policies and practices.

We noted earlier the relevance of "human rights" for the crimes of globalization project. There is, of course, a long history of the promotion and protection of rights within states, and the United States is among Western states that celebrate its long, historical commitment in relation to rights. But "in the US context, rights are still predominantly understood in terms of constitutional law provisions and civil rights/ liberties activism" (Murphy and Whitty 2013: p. 570). Engagement with human rights has an international framework. The recognition of universal human rights has grown exponentially within the current era. For David Garland, "an engagement with human rights is essential for a twenty-first-century criminology that aspires to depth and relevance" (Murphy and Whitty 2013: p. 568). In a similar vein, Joachim Savelsberg (2010: p. 116) writes that "[M]ainstream criminologists must begin to place the issue of humanitarian and human rights crimes high on their agenda and learn from other fields. Simultaneously human rights scholars should avail themselves of criminological insights. There is no time to lose." As a scholarly concern, human rights have been to date principally the province of law and philosophy. Stanley Cohen (1988), among criminologists, was an early promoter of a human rights focus in relation to criminological issues. In the present context criminologists who engage with human rights issues focus principally on genocidal threats (e.g., Hagan and Rymond-Richmond 2009; Savelsberg 2010). But we would argue here that crimes of globalization can certainly be framed as egregious violations of human rights, and should be part of a criminology of human rights project.

Summary

This book addresses "crimes of globalization." Without a widely recognized category of "crimes of globalization of international financial institutions" the harms of these entities have been quite largely invisible to criminologists. Obviously international financial institutions and their activities are not encompassed by traditional criminological typologies. But they also do not readily fit into categories or types created in expanded criminological typologies, including corporate crime, crimes of states, or state-corporate crimes. International financial institutions are not corporations—i.e., private, profit-oriented enterprises. But they are also not states or state-based entities. Rather, they are organizational entities with multiple and important ties to both corporations and states, but also both different from and relatively independent of them. In at least one interpretation, states in the recent era have increasingly transferred rule-making powers to international institutions, broadly defined (Zweifel 2006). The growth of such institutions has been one of the noteworthy developments of the past century. This trend raises many important questions, going forward: To what extent are international institutions overshadowing states in the global arena? To whom are such institutions truly accountable, if they are not direct products of a democratic process, and what is the source of their legitimacy? Whose interests are primarily served by international institutions, and are they on balance a force promoting or subverting social justice globally?

2

WHAT ARE CRIMES OF GLOBALIZATION?

Crimes of globalization are those demonstrably harmful policies and practices of institutions and entities that are specifically a product of the forces of globalization, and that by their very nature occur within a global context. Maureen Cain (2010) applies the term "global crime" to the same harmful policies and practices. Simon Mackenzie (2006) has introduced the term "systematic crime" in his discussion of the broad forms of global harm emanating from the practices of international financial institutions, and their complicity in denying the link between supporting interests of advanced economies and harm in many, if not most, of the global South countries. Although these crimes can involve violations of criminal laws on the state or international level, they may also incorporate harms not specifically addressed by statutory law. The vastly disproportionate influence of elite interests over the formal criminal law is accordingly taken into account in a definition that transcends the boundaries of such law. It is not typically the specific intent of those who engage in crimes of globalization to cause harm. Rather, the devastating harm to vulnerable people in global South countries is a consequence of the skewed priorities of institutions and entities which favor the interests of the powerful and the privileged. But as Maureen Cain (2010) argues, when the harm done could and should have been anticipated—and all too often there is compelling evidence that this is the case—then the term "crime" and not something else can be applied.

The concept of "crimes of globalization" was first put forth in a paper presented at the American Society of Criminology Annual Meeting in 2000 (subsequently published as an article in *Social Justice* in 2002) with the specific title "The World Bank and Crimes of Globalization: A Case Study" by David O. Friedrichs and Jessica Friedrichs. In the Pak Mun dam case, the World Bank helped finance the building of the dam in eastern Thailand in the early 1990s. The process of planning, constructing, and operating this dam was undertaken without obtaining input from the fishermen and villagers who lived along the river. The construction of the dam had a detrimental effect on the environment, flooding the adjacent forests. This effect violated the World Bank's own policies on cultural property destruction. Many edible plants upon which locals were dependent for their sustenance and for income were lost. Villagers who used the river for drinking, bathing, and laundry developed skin rashes. Most importantly, a severe decline in the fish population occurred. As a consequence, the way of life of indigenous fishermen dependent upon abundant fish for food and income was annihilated. The resettlement of the fishermen and compensation for their losses were wholly inadequate. Traditional communities began to disintegrate. Many of those affected by these developments organized protest villages and engaged in other actions calling for the Thai government and the World Bank to take responsibility for the devastation they caused by building the dam, which cost far more than expected and generated far less electricity than had been anticipated.

The concept of crimes of globalization, as originally formulated, was limited to the demonstrably harmful activities of international financial institutions, with a special focus on one of these institutions, the World Bank. However, these crimes intersect with a range of other forms of crime engaged in by powerful entities, including crimes of states, political white collar crime, and state-corporate crime (Friedrichs 2010; Rothe 2009, 2010a,b). Multiple complex interconnections exist between these different types of globalized harm. Accordingly, some refinement of the definition of crimes of globalization seems warranted. In the interest of greater clarity, the notion of crimes of international financial institutions specifically is best classified as a core subtype of the broader category of crimes of globalization. The two principal international financial institutions are the International Monetary Fund, which seeks to maximize financial stability, and the World Bank, primarily focused on promoting development (Woods 2006). The World Trade Organization (WTO) is often aligned with these international financial institutions, and has many parallel attributes and issues, but strictly speaking is an international regulatory entity, with its primary formal mission being to foster trade. In a rapidly changing global economy the roles of the international financial institutions have been increasingly questioned. These institutions have many ties with each other, and the lines of demarcation between their activities can become quite blurred.

Crimes of globalization, transnational crimes and international crimes

The concept of crimes of globalization is not synonymous with two formulations that have received significant recent attention: The "globalization of crime" and "globalization and crime" (e.g., Aas 2007; Friman 2009; Larsen and Smandych 2008). The first of these terms refers broadly to long-standing forms of crime now carried out in an increasingly global context, and the second term refers broadly to the influence of globalization on crime, conventionally defined.

The relationship of crimes of globalization to the familiar but sometimes unclearly invoked terms *transnational crimes* and *international crimes* requires some attention here. There has been a considerable expansion of attention in the recent era to transnational crime (Albanese 2011; Reichel and Albanese 2014; Sheptycki and Wardak 2005). Transnational crime is not a new phenomenon. Pirates, hundreds of years ago, engaged in a form of transnational crime. But as Louise Shelley (2011: p. 3) has observed, "What has changed from the earlier decades of transnational crime is the speed, the extent, and diversity of the actors involved. Globalization has increased the opportunities for criminals, and criminals have been among the major beneficiaries of globalization." New categories of transnational crime have emerged. The literature on transnational crime and justice has principally focused on such crimes as trafficking in persons, migrant smuggling, drugs and counterfeit goods, cybercrime, money laundering, and the transnational organized crime networks that are at the center of many of these forms of transnational criminal activity. Many forms of transnational crime are essentially conventional criminal activities carried out across borders. Some varieties of transnational crime are white collar criminal activities carried out across borders, including: fraudulent marketing, stock manipulation, tax evasion, bribery, environmental pollution, and some forms of money laundering (Grabosky 2009). But as Hazel Croall (2005) has argued, there has been disproportionate attention to the impact of globalization on transnational organized crime, and not that of corporations and financial institutions, although they do far more harm. In this context, she specifically discussed the original Friedrichs and Friedrichs (2002) article on crimes of globalization. The *Handbook of Transnational Crime and Justice* (Reichel and Albanese 2014) reflects the pattern of addressing conventional forms of crime that have become increasingly transnational in character. Michalowski and Kramer's (2014) chapter on transnational environmental crime notes the role of the international financial institutions in shaping economic development and resource usage in the global South, with damaging environmental consequences. But in the rest of this handbook the international financial institutions are only cited in relation to the implementation of the rule of law in global South countries, and in connection with anti-money-laundering initiatives. In effect, in the growing literature on transnational crime, the international financial institutions—to the extent that they are addressed at all—are addressed as entities combatting transnational crime.

We should be clear: transnational organized crime and related forms of transnational crime are hugely harmful and well-deserving of study by criminologists. Our reservation here parallels the critique of disproportionate attention to conventional street crime relative to corporate crime. And secondly, there needs to be more consideration of the complicity of international financial institutions as well as states in transnational crime. H. Richard Friman (2009) has addressed the fact that in many ways states—which often claim to be combatting transnational crime—in fact facilitate and enable the activities of global criminal networks.

Organized crime has long had transnational dimensions. The processes of globalization have been transforming some dimensions of such crime, with these transnational dimensions increasingly central to the operation of emerging forms of organized crime. Certainly the threat of transnational or global terrorism is substantial, but the argument can be made that it also has received disproportionate attention relative to other forms of transnational or global harm. Especially since 9/11, there has been a huge amount of attention to transnational or global terrorism.

International crimes are best conceived of as international core crimes or violations of international law, which in their generic form (e.g., genocide, war crimes, crimes against humanity, and massive violations of human rights) have a long history. Such crimes have often been committed within national boundaries, but are increasingly carried out globally. International crimes are most typically thought of as crimes of states, but may also be committed by insurgencies, militias, and other parties. Corporations—and increasingly multinational corporations— are also complicit in international crimes. For example, some of the corporations operating in Nazi Germany and its occupied territories played a role in the Holocaust, serving as a classic case of such crimes. In the more recent era such corporations as Blackwater (XE), Sandline and Halliburton have been accused of violations of international law (Rothe 2009). The conditions of globalization produce expanding opportunities for such crime.

The lines of demarcation between crimes of globalization, transnational crimes, and international crimes are sometimes fluid and complex. But the key actors typically involved, and the bodies of law violated, tend to be different.

Any coherent discussion of "crimes of globalization" must also address the interconnections with two other forms of crime: state-corporate crime and crimes of states.

Crimes of globalization, state-corporate crime and crimes of states

The crimes of international financial institutions (IFIs) have a generic relationship to *state-corporate crimes* insofar as they are cooperative ventures involving public sector and private sector entities, and in some respects are hybrid public/private sector entities. The literature on state-corporate crime (e.g., Michalowski and Kramer 2006) has focused on crimes arising out of cooperative ventures involving states and corporations. The relationship between crimes of globalization and state-corporate crimes are heavily intertwined, yet rarely are these connections made in the state-corporate crime literature (see Friedrichs and Rothe, forthcoming). In one sense, crimes of globalization could be characterized as a neglected, cognate form of such crime: that is, state-international financial institution crime.

Altogether, the intersection of business and government has led to increased cases of a "globalized criminality." In the recent era Western states as well as corporations have promoted neo-liberalism or a supposed "free market" model for the global political economy. Within such an environment the crimes of globalization of international financial institutions are intertwined with crimes of states and of corporations. The policies and practices of the international financial institutions are largely driven by the global agenda of powerful states such as the United States. These states in turn are strongly oriented toward supporting the interests of corporations.

In many of the global South countries corrupt political oligarchs facilitate the promotion of the global state-corporate agenda, despite it being largely at odds with the interest of their citizens. Cases of such corrupt practices have been especially pronounced and well-documented in the case of sub-Saharan countries of Africa, such as the Democratic Republic of Congo, Rwanda, and Senegal (Rothe 2010b). But altogether these corrupt practices are a global phenomenon.

Having clarified some of the intertwinement between and distinctions of the various forms of crimes noted above and crimes of globalization, it seems pertinent to provide a brief overview of the international financial institutions themselves.

International financial institutions

From the onset, the international financial institutions were designed to maintain growth of the world economies and provide currency stabilization loans to alleviate any major economic crisis, and development loans to foster and promote a neo-liberal laissez-faire economic system (Jackson 2012; Woods 2006; Zweifel 2006). The *International Monetary Fund* came into formal existence at the Bretton Woods conference in 1945, when 29 member countries signed its Articles of Agreement. Its first official operations began in 1947 with France as the first borrowing country. During the late 1950s and 1960s membership in the International Monetary Fund began to expand as many colonized territories gained their independence. Since the International Monetary Fund was first established, its stated purposes have remained largely unchanged, but its operations such as surveillance, financial assistance, and technical assistance have changed in focus somewhat throughout its history. In 1986, the institution created a loan program, the Structural Adjustment Facility, which was then succeeded by the Enhanced Structural Adjustment Facility (1987). Since these changes, it has expanded to include programs such as the Poverty Reduction and Growth Facility.

The International Monetary Fund (IMF) today is an organization of 188 member countries and claims to "foster global monetary cooperation, secure financial stability, facilitate international trade, promote high employment and sustainable economic growth, and reduce poverty around the world" (International Monetary Fund 2013a: p. 1). However, we will be making the case that the International Monetary Fund is in fact complicit in much harm and crime in developing countries. It continues to "encourage" countries to adopt what it believes to be "sound economic policies or reforms," or what most commentators refer to as neo-liberal economics. Such economic reforms are imposed on borrowing states supposedly to create socio-economic conditions more conducive to economic health and growth. These can include, but are not limited to, opening government-owned industries to privatization, removal of tariffs, health care fees, acceptance of currency re-evaluations and reductions in social or other governmental spending programs in ways determined by the lenders. In most cases, there has been "a strong focus on fiscal thrift to which most other concerns are subordinated" (Torrance and Lochery 2008: p. 3). This leads to a broad range of harms for citizens of global South countries.

The *World Bank*, formally the International Bank for Reconstruction and Development (IBRD), was established at the Bretton Woods Conference in 1944 to help stabilize and rebuild economies ravaged by World War II. Eventually it shifted its focus to an emphasis on aiding global South countries. The World Bank is not a "bank" in the commonly used sense of the term. Rather, it is a specialized financial agency, composed of 184 member countries. Conceived during World War II, it initially helped to rebuild postwar Europe. In 1947, its first loan of $250 million went to France for reconstruction.

Once its original mission of postwar European reconstruction was finished, the World Bank turned its lending practices to development issues. Its rhetoric was often focused on human rights, human dignity, and infrastructure development, but its operational concerns strongly focused on producing returns for investors. Through the 1970s and 1980s, global South countries were frequently unable to meet repayment demands. Therefore, during the 1980s the Bank went through an extensive period that focused on issues related to macroeconomics and debt rescheduling. During the latter part of the 1980s, social and environmental issues assumed center stage and an increasingly vocal and active civil society in Europe and the Americas accused the Bank of failing to observe its own policies in some high-profile projects. The World Bank often did not respond directly to the critiques and more human rights focused concerns of these populations, though it did begin to consider the need for debt restructuring. Yet, as with other actions, the World Bank did not simply accede to the vocal minorities that demanded global policy changes. In return for debt reallocation or admission into forgiveness programs, it demanded that macro-structural political and economic changes occur within the debtor nations. In many cases, the World Bank also required recipient countries to adopt certain political measures, such as policies that would foster "democracy," by which it meant opening state holdings to private ownership. Votes allocated to member countries regarding specific programs are linked to the size of its share-holding. Initial membership in the World Bank gives equal voting rights, but there are also additional votes. These votes depend on financial contributions to the organization by member states, implying undemocratic decision-making. Altogether, as we will document further on, the World Bank has been complicit in much harm and crime in global South countries.

More recently, the World Bank became a Group, encompassing five closely associated development institutions: the International Bank for Reconstruction and Development (IBRD), the International Development Association (IDA), the International Finance Corporation (IFC), the Multilateral Investment Guarantee Agency (MIGA), and the International Centre for Settlement of Investment Disputes (ICSID). Since the mid- to late 1990s, the World Bank utilizes the Private Sector Development (PSD) as its strategy to promote privatization in the global South wherein other strategies must be coordinated with the push towards privatization. The Bank makes low-interest loans to governments of its member states and to private "development" projects backed by those governments with the stated aim to benefit the citizens of those countries.

Today the World Bank is a large, international operation with more than 10,000 employees, 184 member states, and annual loans of $170 billion (Strom 2011).

In addition to providing financing, the World Bank offers advice and assistance to countries on almost every aspect of economic development. For the World Bank's fiscal year 2013 (June 2012 to June 2013), the commitments for the International Development Association (IDA)—the

TABLE 2.1 The World Bank Group commitments to loans by divisions

World Bank Group	Fiscal Year 2013 (billions of U.S. dollars)	Fiscal Year 2012 (billions of U.S. dollars)
International Bank for Reconstruction and Development (IBRD)	15.2	20.6
International Development Association (IDA)	16.3	14.7
International Finance Corporation	18.3	15.4
Multilateral Investment Guarantee Agency	2.8	2.7
Total	52.6	53.4

Bank's fund for the "poorest" countries—and the International Finance Corporation (the arm of the Bank promoting private business ventures in global South countries) were at an all-time high.

International financial institutions: in sum

The World Bank was established at the Bretton Woods conference in 1944, along with the International Monetary Fund, at the behest of dominant Western states, with little input from developing countries (Bretton Woods Project 2013). It is disproportionately influenced or manipulated by elite economic institutions and entities—e.g., transnational mining companies—and has been characterized as an agent of global capital. In most of the global South countries, World Bank officials deal primarily with the political and economic elites of those countries with little direct attention to the perspectives and needs of indigenous peoples (Babb 2009; Goldman 2005; Weaver 2008). It has loaned money to ruthless military dictatorships engaged in murder and torture and denied loans to democratic governments subsequently overthrown by the military. It has favored strong dictatorships over struggling democracies because it believes that the former are more able to introduce and see through the unpopular reforms their loan payments require. The World Bank and the International Monetary Fund borrowers typically are political elites of global South countries and their cronies, although repaying the debt becomes the responsibility of these countries' citizens, most of whom do not benefit from the loans.

Ultimately, more money flows out of the borrowing countries to the World Bank and the International Monetary Fund than the reverse (Goldman 2005; Jackson 2012). The privileged in the global South countries have been the principal beneficiaries of the World Bank and International Monetary Fund loans, not poor people in those countries. The officials within the international financial institutions have little, if any, direct contact with the indigenous peoples most affected by its projects.

The World Bank and the International Monetary Fund have been targets of much criticism, especially in the recent era. They have been characterized as paternalistic, secretive, and counterproductive in terms of their claimed goals of improving people's lives. They have been called fundamentally hypocritical due to the gap between the professed objectives for the projects they support and the actual outcomes (Weaver 2008). They have been charged with complicity in policies with genocidal consequences, with exacerbating ethnic conflict, with increasing the gap between rich and poor, with fostering immense ecological and environmental damage, with neglecting agriculture crucial to survival in many of the global South countries, and with the callous displacement of vast numbers of indigenous people in these countries from their original homes and communities.

In the wake of these widespread criticisms of the ineffectiveness and harmful consequences of the structural adjustment programs and other programs imposed on global South countries by the World Bank and the International Monetary Fund, a shift to poverty reduction was announced as a new goal in the more recent period (Abouharb and Cingarelli 2006; Brady 2010). Although the World Bank continues to identify the reduction of poverty as a primary goal, a former official of the World Bank questions its capacity to do so (Shaman 2009). Since 9/11 in particular, foreign aid overall has been directed principally toward fighting terrorism, not toward alleviating poverty, and the World Bank's anti-poverty campaign has become increasingly marginalized. The sad irony in all of this is the perception of many observers that poverty in the global South is one of the primary forces driving international terrorism. Since the global economic crisis of 2008, it has been estimated that an additional fifty million people will be locked into poverty at least through 2015 (Chan 2010). If the World Bank and the International Monetary Fund are not directly responsible for this circumstance, they have also not been clearly effective counter-forces. Some of the issues noted in this summary section have been the focus of several research projects and articles by scholars of crimes of globalization. The following section provides an overview of the cases of crimes committed by the international financial institutions directly and indirectly.

Overview of previous research

In the wake of the original crimes of globalization article focusing upon the World Bank and the case of the Pak Mun dam, a number of criminologists have applied the concept of crimes of globalization to other circumstances. For example, Rothe *et al.* (2006) conducted research that explored the interrelations between the International Monetary Fund and the World Bank, and legacies of colonialism along with foreign policies that set the stage for large-scale atrocities and crimes of states. Exploring the circumstances leading to the sinking of the ferry *Le Joola*, the authors demonstrated that the state of Senegal itself had core liability for this maritime tragedy, with its dramatic loss of lives. The government readily admitted its errors and several ministers either stepped down or were removed from their positions. However, despite unequivocal governmental responsibility, Rothe *et al.* advanced the case that the sinking could not be characterized simply as a case of state crime. Rather, a thorough investigation and analysis of the reasons and forces behind the *Le Joola* sinking suggested that international financial institutions bore some clear culpability for the disaster. In response to Structural Adjustment Programs (SAPs) imposed by the International Monetary Fund, the Senegalese government was forced to cut spending in many areas. These spending cuts extended to ferry programs central to transportation in Senegal, especially in relation to its geographic location. This had a direct impact on the upkeep and return of the *Le Joola* to open waters. The ferry capsized with only one of its two engines functioning, resulting in the deaths of 1863 passengers. This was the second largest maritime disaster in history. Most crucially, the authors of this study demonstrated why scholars need to examine the criminogenic effects of policies and practices of international financial institutions in developing countries such as Senegal. These policies and practices privilege capitalistic profit over human lives and a better quality of life for people in much of the global South. Accordingly, this is crime against vulnerable human beings.

An article by Rothe *et al.* (2009) took a parallel approach, exploring the role of international financial institution policies in the conditions leading to the Rwandan genocide in 1994. While the World Bank and the International Monetary Fund did not seek to instigate economic collapse or to promote genocide, their policies and their systematic inattention in Rwanda set the stage for political and economic disaster as well as the genocide itself. The authors suggested that these international financial institutions knowingly violated their own standards, as well as international human rights principles. Through the imposition of harsh conditions tied to their financial aid, they facilitated criminal activities on a massive scale.

In an article published in 2008, Ezeonu and Koku also adopted the crimes of globalization concept. They demonstrated the key contributing role played by the neo-liberal policies of international financial institutions in sub-Saharan Africa, in expanding the vulnerability of people in this region to HIV infection. They called for more systematic criminological attention to the victimization of people in developing countries as a consequence of the promotion of neo-liberal policies and practices in an increasingly globalized world (see also Ezeonu 2008).

In a similar vein, Rothe (2010a,b) has provided an analysis of the complicity of international financial institutions in heightened levels of corruption and the suppression or violation of human rights in many of the global South countries. Analyzing such complicity seems especially important given that these institutions claim to be engaged in combating corruption in developing countries, including those linked to transnational and multinational corporations. The anti-corruption initiatives include threatening to withhold much-needed economic aid and loans in the absence of action taken against corrupt activities in these countries. Rothe has illustrated the specific role of the international financial institutions in the illegal expropriation of the rich natural resources of the Democratic Republic of Congo by the neighboring countries of Uganda and Rwanda. Beyond theft on a grand scale, Rwandan and Ugandan state forces and militias also engaged in especially atrocious human rights violations conducted against civilian populations, including forced labor, systematic rape and widespread killing. Through their funding of African states engaged in crimes against both their own citizens and those of neighboring countries, the international financial institutions bear some responsibility for these crimes.

Parallel circumstances have arisen in other parts of the world. Stanley (2009) has analyzed the role of the international financial institutions in Indonesia. They directed some $30 billion to the Suharto regime, despite its known record of massive corruption, false accounting, and a militaristic appropriation of aid funds. As the World Bank's focus was on supporting Indonesia, the state was able to use funds supposedly intended to reduce poverty in its brutal campaign against civilians in the state of Timor-Leste. This campaign had as its purpose terrorizing people to deter them from voting for independence from Indonesia. One could identify many other cases in Asia and other parts of the world where the international financial institutions have been complicit in supporting corrupt, authoritarian regimes and facilitating their massive violations of human rights.

The concept of crimes of globalization has also been adopted in relation to forms of crime that occur in the context of globalization but do not specifically involve the international financial institutions. Wright and Muzzatti (2007) have addressed the global restructuring of agriculture and food systems—agri-food globalization—with some specific attention to the victimization of huge numbers of animals: for example, 58,000 sheep stranded at sea for almost three months in 2003, in violation of animal welfare law. Altogether, policies and practices relating to the global restructuring of agriculture and food systems were driving up food prices, pushing tens of millions of people towards hunger and starvation. The global North countries' farm subsidies were driving large numbers of farmers in the global South countries into desperate circumstances, to the advantage of corporate and high finance interests in the wealthy countries of the world. Giant American agribusiness corporations such as Cargill and Archer Daniels Midland (ADM), through their exploitative activities, were contributing to the ongoing suffering on many levels in those countries (North 2011).

Maureen Cain (2010) addresses the notion of a global state, and in this context adopts the term "global crime" for the harms caused by international financial institutions. Drawing on the case of Trinidad and Tobago, Cain attributes increases in instrumental crimes (e.g., property crimes) and self-assertive crimes (e.g., crimes of violence) to policies mandated by international financial institutions. More generally, Cain suggests that on a global scale the policies of these institutions in highly indebted countries have many criminogenic effects, including: heightened levels of poverty, privatization of natural resources, reduced social services, and other recognized structurally negative mandated outcomes.

The notion of crimes of globalization has also been implicitly adopted by some authors who are not criminologists, and who are addressing a broad public audience. A book by John Perkins (2005), entitled *Confessions of an Economic Hit Man*, became a bestseller following its publication in 2005. He defined economic hit men (EHM) as "highly paid professionals who cheat countries around the globe out of trillions of dollars" (Perkins 2005: p. ix). In his case, as an employee of an international consulting firm, Perkins claims to have participated in a range of activities involved in funneling funds from international financial institutions and international aid organizations into the hands of major transnational corporations and a small number of wealthy and influential families in the global South countries. Economic hit men are engaged in persuading global South leaders to become part of a vast global network that ultimately serves the interest of U.S.-based corporations and U.S. businesses generally, at the enormous expense of the people of the developing countries. In a subsequent book, *The Secret History of the American Empire*, Perkins (2007) further explored some of these themes. Although these two books have been criticized as self-dramatizing, they may well have succeeded in raising the consciousness of new audiences about crimes of globalization.

In *A Game as Old as Empire: The Secret World of Economic Hit Men and the Web of Global Corruption* (Hiatt 2007: p. 20), a book inspired by the Perkins' bestseller, various authors address aspects of "the corporatocracy" ("the powerful people who run the world's biggest corporations, the most powerful governments, and history's first truly global empire"). These authors addressed such matters as the hundreds of billions of dollars that the global South countries spend annually for servicing their debt, the world of offshore banking, the expropriation of Africa's oil wealth, the role of export credit agencies in boosting overseas sales for multinational corporations, and the mirage of debt relief.

More recently, Ross Jackson (2012) published the book *Occupy World Street: A Global Roadmap for Radical Economic and Political Reform* that not only suggests a vision for the future global economic structure, but also addresses the corruption and inevitable fall of the current global financial system, of which the International Monetary Fund and World Bank have primacy as the major drivers of the neo-liberal economic agenda. Showing the downside to the dogma of "development," poverty reduction, and stability, Jackson makes a clear argument that the present system is not sustainable.

One need only monitor the daily news to see some of the ongoing issues associated with the ideology, policies, and practices of the international financial institutions. Crimes of globalization that have occurred in the past and continue to occur today have vast costs for the citizens of most of the global South countries. These crimes have a hugely detrimental impact on the increasingly fragile global environment. The following chapter presents several contemporary and concurrent crimes of globalization perpetrated, directly and indirectly, by these international financial institutions.

3

SOME CURRENT CASES OF CRIMES OF GLOBALIZATION

International financial institutions' policies and practices impact negatively on the broader global system. They also cause identifiable, specific harm with projects undertaken in individual countries of the global South. In the previous chapter some such projects were addressed. But these projects were undertaken years ago, in many cases prior to high-profile protest demonstrations and other forms of criticisms—in numerous books and articles—directed at the international financial institutions and their projects. These institutions have been acutely sensitive to the criticism directed towards them, and have instituted new policies and goal objectives. Unfortunately, it does not follow from this that crimes of globalization are a thing of the past. In this chapter we identify some ongoing as well as some new cases of crimes of globalization.

The imposition of odious debt

Debt has come to be recognized as a huge problem in the world today (Graeber 2011; Hyman 2011; Kuttner 2013). Admittedly, state governments—and especially large, complex modern governments—

have long been dependent upon taking on debt to function effectively and to provide citizens with services and benefits that are essential. However, much of the debt taken on by less economically empowered countries—or the countries of the global South—are here characterized in relation to crimes of globalization.

First, the debt is taken on by these countries—often (although not always) through the international financial institutions—on behalf of "development" and "growth." As we previously mentioned in Chapter 1, these are not truly neutral terms (Black 2007; Toussaint and Millet 2010). Development and growth are defined in ways that are skewed to the interests of transnational corporations based in the most empowered countries—namely Western states and the global North, and more broadly these countries and their citizens. This is not to deny that some segments of the citizenry in the more economically weak countries benefit from debt-supported "development" and economic growth. But overall the evidence on the effects of debt taken on by these countries can be shown to fund projects which not only fail to improve life for most citizens of the countries (and especially the disadvantaged citizens of these countries), but in some cases intensify their poverty and destroy their traditional way of life.

The core decisions relating to the debt are made by the international financial institutions, other Western governmental entities (e.g., the U.S. Department of Treasury), and consortiums of big banks in these countries (i.e., the Paris Club and the London Club, as they are known). It is their priorities—to insure debt repayment, to open up borders to capitalist enterprises, and to extend to political allies privileged treatment—that guide these decisions (Toussaint and Millet 2010). In one recent year over half a trillion dollars was paid by debtor countries to service their external and private debt, with some $800 billion annually repaid each year by public authorities in these countries.

Altogether, debt has risen sharply in the global South countries since the mid-1990s, with the international financial institutions playing a key role in this situation (Toussaint and Millet 2010) (see Appendix A for an account of these countries' total debt and debt to gross national product ratio). These debt obligations have a crippling and devastating impact on the economies of the global South countries and on the ordinary citizens of these countries. In the words of one commentator: "The long history of economic exploitation and domination by foreign capital has impoverished much of the African continent. The capitalists have extracted billions in profits and managed to leave the exploited nations hundreds of billions in debt" (Kanowicz 2010: p. 127). Such systemic exploitation is surely increasingly visible and a source of festering resentment and anger within the exploited nations.

The international financial institutions have contributed in a fundamental way to the debt crisis that has crippled the economies of many global South countries since the early 1980s. Yes, corruption, megalomania and the lack of democracy within these countries has contributed substantially to the dismal state of their economies, but there is much reason to believe that international financial institutions based in the West triggered the debt crisis in the global South countries (Toussaint and Millet 2010). The huge burden of paying off debt imposed by the international financial institutions and other global North entities has fallen very disproportionately on the shoulders of ordinary citizens of most of the global South countries, despite the fact that they have not benefited or profited—for the most part—from this debt. By some estimations, even though repayments on such debts may exceed three or four times the amount of the original debt, due to these repayments being directed almost entirely to interests payments, the principal of the original debt remains in place (Graeber 2011). Furthermore, "the International Monetary Fund basically acted as the world's debt enforcers —'You might say, the high-finance equivalent of the guys who come to break your legs'" (Graeber 2011: p. 2). The International Monetary Fund works in cooperation with the World Bank and such entities as the Paris Club and the London Club to insure that repayment of debt takes priority over other concerns and that the global South countries adopt policies that favor their interests and those of rich Western and global North countries overall (Toussaint and Millet 2010). These policies include deregulation of the market in line with the promotion of the Western neo-liberal economic agenda, and such deregulation has also contributed to an enormous increase in the internal public debt of countries in the global South (Toussaint and Millet

2010). On multiple different levels, then, citizens of these countries are adversely affected by the policies of the international financial institutions.

As previously noted, the Structural Adjustment Programs imposed by the World Bank and the International Monetary Fund lead specifically to: cuts in social spending (including on basic health and education expenditures), export-driven agricultural policies which produce a reduction of basic food crops and a loss of food sovereignty in these countries, and a range of other policies that exacerbate poverty and have worsened living conditions for hundreds of millions of people in these countries (Toussaint and Millet 2010). The consequent explosion of food prices in the global South countries surely plays a role in the fact that approximately one third of the children in these countries are undernourished. Some one billion people have inadequate access to water, and some 2.6 billion lack basic sanitation (Toussaint and Millet 2010). The spread of malaria and tuberculosis in these countries has been linked specifically to the policies of the international financial institutions (Toussaint and Millet 2010). The fact that tens of millions in sub-Saharan Africa have been infected with the AIDS virus, and several million a year die from it, has also been specifically characterized as a crime of globalization, in relation to international financial institutions' policies (Ezeonu 2008; Toussaint and Millet 2010). Children in debtor countries, in significant numbers, have died in relation to inflated food prices. Furthermore, each day more than 30,000 children die of easily curable diseases, and each year 500,000 women die of pregnancy or childbirth-related complications (Toussaint and Millet 2010: p. 34). These deaths can surely be linked, at least in part, to the mandated policies of the international financial institutions that require cuts in health care programs. The international financial institutions expect desperately poor people in debt-burdened countries to pay for basic services, including hospital-delivery of babies and "even a bucket of water" (Black 2007: p. 85). The debt taken on by these countries is contracted for by corrupt political leaders who proceed to siphon off a huge fraction of the debt for themselves, or to benefit relatives and associates within the private sector elite class within their country. The ordinary citizens have no input in the commitments made on their behalf to take on debt or on the conditions attached to the debt.

In Nigeria, as just one specific example, the World Bank and the International Monetary Fund imposed loans "by stipulation" to fund drilling, extraction and oil processing in Nigeria (Kanowicz 2010: p. 125). Four-fifths of the oil extraction projects have been export-oriented (i.e., primarily beneficial to the global North and Western countries in particular). Meanwhile, between 1970 and 2010 Nigeria's debt rose from $1 billion to $30 billion. Beyond the issue of debt there are the environmental, cultural, and economic harms that occur through the support and funding by international financial institutions and resource extraction, as was the case with Nigeria.

Mineral resource extraction

Over the past decade, international financial institutions have "actively promoted and financed the liberalization of the hydrocarbon and mining sectors of national economies across the globe" stating that the "public-private collaborations among governments, international financial institutions and multinational corporations will enhance social well-being by eradicating poverty, promoting sustainable forms of economic development, protecting the environment and advancing the rights of indigenous peoples" (Sawyer and Gomez 2008: p. 1). While such statements are firmly grounded in the neo-liberal ideology of development and open markets, they more often than not remain unchallenged within the institutions and the promotion of resource extraction continues to escalate (see Appendix B for a list of country resource extraction projects under the World Bank transparency initiative).

The majority of resource extraction projects are funded through an arm of the World Bank—the International Finance Corporation—that is the largest global "development" institution focused exclusively on the private sector. This is the case with the mining projects as well. The Ahafo mine project in Ghana included a $75 million investment loan (A equity loan) and a $10 million secured loan (B loan) to Newmont, one of the largest U.S.-based multinational mining corporations. Likewise, the Simandou mine, Guinea, included an investment of a $35 million loan to Rio Tinto and a $15 million equity loan to Nyota for the Tulu Kapi mine, Ethiopia. Another current project is a $12 billion investment to develop a copper and gold mine at Oyu Tolgi, in the southern region of Mongolia. The latter project is said to be a cornerstone of Mongolia's economic development. In May 2013, the International Finance Corporation announced a Can $5 million investment in Unigold Incorporated for gold and base metal exploration for the Neita project in the Dominican Republic for a "future development plan" stating that the "IFC will work with the company to ensure that exploration and any subsequent mine development is carried out in an environmentally and socially sustainable manner" (International Finance Corporation 2011: p. 1). While perhaps a well-intended statement, the development and operation of open-pit mining and resource extraction has not been associated with environmental or social sustainability.

Consider a few case-specific examples. The Newmont Mining Corporation was awarded an International Finance Corporation loan of $125 million in January 2006 to develop the first of the Ahafo open-pit gold mines (Ahafo South) in a heavy agricultural region northwest of Ghana's capital, Accra. To get to the production level, Newmont "established a mill, waste rock disposal facilities, water storage facility, tailings storage facility, environmental control dams, haul roads and other mine infrastructure" (Owusu-Koranteng 2010: p. 2). Newmont currently operates four open-pit mines at Ahafo with the reserves contained in eleven constructed pits. Production of the fourth pit, Amoma, started in October 2010 (Newmont 2013). The project covers "774 square kilometres which comprises the overall mining license. The open pits are the most visible land disturbance but account for only 14% of the total land use. Stockpiles and waste dumps account for 35%, water and tailings reservoirs 34% and facilities, roads and other infrastructure 17%" (Newmont 2011: p. 51).

Beyond the social and economic harms, including the displacement of 10,000 indigenous people, the environmental harms are numerous. There are normal environmental impacts and harms that result from open-pit gold mining, beginning with the destruction of the environment at the mine site, vast craters, and damage to the surrounding ecological system. Toxic mine drainage is commonly associated with gold mining. The process of digging up the rock can set off chemical reactions that produce a lot of acid-generating sulfides and leach toxic metals such as sulfuric acid and arsenic which can run off into lakes, streams and rivers, posing serious risk to fish and other life forms dependent on the water outlets. Mine drainage is a common problem. Once the process of extracting the gold from the ore begins, there is also the issue of mercury through the roasting process or dousing the ore in cyanide that can result in nitrates being produced which can contaminate water. Gold tailing ponds, such as the four at the Ahofa mine site, are "chock-full of contaminants such as arsenic, antimony, residual cyanide and mercury . . . These tailings can stay toxic for centuries" (Rastogi 2010: p. 1).

At the Ahofa mine, Newmont planned for cyanide to be discharged into specifically made tailing ponds (where the material that's left over once the ore has been processed is held) without a cyanide kill process, thus allowing residual cyanide at levels above water quality. As a result, seepage into groundwater occurs. While claiming the process of photo degradation would kill the cyanide, Newmont failed to acknowledge that this form of degradation is only effective at or near the surface of the pond. The waste rock facilities were constructed with low permeability materials and the use and diversion of water storage dams has resulted in a loss for the surrounding indigenous people and the natural flow of the ecological order. As noted in the environmental assessment by Center for Science and Public Participation (2005: p. 1) "water withdrawal for mine activities is discussed primarily in terms of water needed by the mine for its operations . . . [not] the impact of withdrawal on natural resources and non-mine consumptive uses (such as drinking water, agriculture, etc."

Over the course of the past seven years, since the initial onset of the first mine development process began, the mine has had two known cyanide leaks with the largest occurring in October 2009, causing mass environmental harms by poisoning local water supplies and killing scores of fish (No Dirty Gold 2010). There have been two floods that occurred from the Control Dam 2 (ECD 2), one in September 2007 that was the result of the spillway being opened and in July 2010. The sewage disposal at the Newmont operation has also been a concern because of the overflow of sewage into a stream and the river causing pollution in the River Subri, affecting the communities of Ahunukrom,

Kwaku Addaikrom, Akorongo, Kwameduanekrom as well as the general ecological system.

Despite the demonstrably harmful effects of its mineral extraction operations, Newmont continues to expand with additional mines in Ghana. For example, the Akyem project is centrally located in a forest reserve in the Birim North District of the Eastern Region of Ghana. This mine, when completed, will destroy roughly "340 acres of tropical forest along with a fourth of the forest left in the Ajenjua Bepo Forest Reserve" (Cardhoff 2011: p. 1). Given the location, the potential for environmental harms that often result from mines-acid drainage, water contamination with heavy metals and cyanide that can leak, is substantial. The impact of this mine on local and global biodiversity raises serious concerns over the professed commitment to the environment. The real priority is the maintenance of free markets and maximizing profits for private enterprises.

While we have discussed the environmental (potential and real) impact and harms related to Newmont's mining projects, this is not specific to one corporation. It is an endemic problem that extends to all open-pit mining projects. Consider the Tarkwa gold mine in the Wassa West District of Ghana, funded by the International Finance Corporation and operated by Gold Fields Ghana. Here another large environmental disaster occurred when large amounts of mine waste went into the Asuman River (2003), contaminating it with cyanide and other heavy metals. In this case, nearly all forms of life in the river and its branches died, including local birds that drank from the water. Furthermore, these instances of spills leave residue that could potentially remain for decades, posing long-term environmental and health issues.

Pipeline projects

Other high-profile projects such as the Chad-Cameroon Pipeline highlight the World Bank's direct and harmful involvement in areas of violations of human rights, indigenous rights, ecological systems, and unsustainable projects. In June 2000 the World Bank approved financing for what was a highly controversial project: the Chad-Cameroon Petroleum Development and Pipeline Project (Badgley 2010). This was a

650-mile pipeline to carry oil from Chad to Kribi to Bume to an offshore loading terminal off the coast of Cameroon. As one commentator notes:

> Despite an international campaign to stop the project that brought together more than 80 environmental and human rights groups, the Board of Directors of the Bank voted unanimously to support it, arguing that oil development represented Chad's best—perhaps only—chance at escaping its crushing poverty.
>
> (Badgley 2010: p. 2)

With the sanctioning and funding of the World Bank, Exxon Mobil and its partners, Chevron and Petronas, began the $4.2 billion pipeline project. The indigenous population that lived along the path of the pipeline was promised employment and grand benefits from the construction of the pipeline. However, as with other World Bank projects, the benefits for local communities are negligible at best; the harmful impact is considerable. Many indigenous people lost their land without compensation, beyond the value of the crops they were growing; others lost their livelihood. In Bume, Cameroon, the reef of the coast—once rich with fish and for some 80 percent of the population the basis of their livelihood—was destroyed. With the removal of the reef, fish no longer had their normal habitat and the local economy plummeted further. The pipeline cut through the rain forest, disrupting the ecosystem upon which the indigenous people in those regions depended. Crews also left roads and water sources damaged and not repaired. To date, they remain as they were left by Exxon and the World Bank. Cameroon had also expected great benefits from the pipeline project. However, the compensation for the 500-mile passage through the state and the prime offshore site did not reap the anticipated benefits. Cameroon only received transit fees without an indexation to inflation or to the price of a barrel. There have also been two known offshore oil leaks, one in 2007 and the other in 2010. These oil leaks have impacted negatively on the local shore villages.

The "villagization" program

Other serious harms include the violation of human rights through programs supported and funded by the international financial institutions.

Consider the "villagization" program currently in place in Ethiopia, funded by the World Bank through the World Bank's Promoting Basic Services (PBS) Program (a $2 billion program established in 2006). This project is said to create new development by relocating indigenous populations to centralized areas with better infrastructure, allowing for the use of the lands for foreign investment. The reality is that much of the land taken from the indigenous population is turned over to foreign interests. A village woman who was relocated to Carmie when government officials came to her farmland was told: "We have some projects to implement here. [Saudi investor name withheld] needs to use this area for a market so you must go" (Human Rights Watch 2013: p. 30). Other villagers displaced from the Baro River region provided similar testimony to Human Rights Watch.

Between 2010 and the time of this writing (July 2013), the Ethiopian government has been actively relocating roughly 1.5 million indigenous people in five regions under a "villagization" program: 500,000 in Somali region, 500,000 in Afar region, 225,000 in Benishangul-Gumuz, and 225,000 in Gambella (Human Rights Watch 2013). In the Western Gambella region, the first region to be "villagized," the main vehicle for achieving development objectives included the process of relocation and land reallocation, as envisioned under the World Bank project. The region of Gambella is endowed with high quality soil, abundant water supplies, and forest cover in many areas, along with other natural resources. It is composed of roughly 307,000 people. Yet, the relocation process has been marred by violence—from rape to torture—and populations being left in remote pseudo-villages that lack basic infrastructure and in some cases water supplies. An Anuak elder in Abobo Woreda stated to a Human Rights Watch interviewer (2012b: p. 25):

> We want the world to hear that government brought the Anuak people here to die. They brought us no food, they gave away our land to the foreigners so we can't even move back. On all sides the land is given away, so we will die here in one place.

In the Gambella region, Human Rights Watch (2013) "found that the relocation process has been marred by intimidation and violence . . . State security forces have threatened, arbitrarily arrested, and assaulted people when implementing 'villagization.'" One member of the indigenous population stated in an interview with Human Rights Watch workers that "[s]oldiers came and asked me why I refused to be relocated . . . They started beating me until my hands were broken . . . I ran to tell [my father] what had happened, but the soldiers followed me. My father and I ran away . . . I heard the sound of gunfire." Human Rights Watch stated that this witness ran and hid from the soldiers in nearby bushes, separating himself from his father, and when he returned the following day, he found that his father had been killed. In another case an interviewee stated:

> The government with the soldiers and elders called us for a meeting where we were told we were to be moved . . . Those that spoke up are considered "inciters," and five of them were arrested . . . They were in prison for between 20 days and one month and released on the condition they do not speak against villagization.
>
> (Human Rights Watch 2012b: p. 29)

A person from the Dimma Woreda region said: "People left their crops behind then tried to return. Those who refused to go had their houses burned down by soldiers. Crops were destroyed. In [the village], where there were many mangoes and some sugar cane, government soldiers burned 100 houses" (Human Rights Watch 2013: p. 29).

The link between the World Bank's support for this villagization and subsequent violence and violations of human rights is direct and indirect. The project funds are being used to pay salaries of government officials who are violating basic human rights of the indigenous population, torturing, killing, raping those that refuse to leave or are in political opposition to the regime and/or program. The overall lack of oversight and continued funding amidst formal complaints by non-governmental organizations and groups of indigenous populations make the World Bank complicit in these crimes of globalization.

Dam projects

There are other recent examples of crimes of globalization in African countries. The concept of "crimes of globalization" originated in response to a World Bank–funded dam project in Thailand. Despite the substantial criticism directed at this and other dam projects they continue in some cases to be funded. For example, the World Bank's Board of Directors approved a $684 million loan, July 2012, for a 1,000-kilometer transmission line to supply power to Kenya from Ethiopia's contentious Gibe III hydroelectric dam project. The World Bank Board of Directors originally refused to fund the dam project, due to professed concerns that the rights of the indigenous population would be violated and serious environmental harms would occur. The World Bank in the recent era has become more sensitive to widespread criticism of its funding of dam projects in developing countries. But due to pressure on the World Bank by vested interest groups, the Bank ultimately approved the loan. The construction of the Gibe III dam project has already been associated with many human rights abuses and the devastation of the local ecosystem in Ethiopia and Kenya's Lake Turkina, the world's largest desert lake. The Ethiopian government is planning on taking an additional 245,000 hectares of land downstream from the Gibe III dam site for a state-run irrigated sugar plantation. This plan will have serious consequences for the indigenous population, including forced relocations and loss of land for their own agriculture and grazing. These two projects will significantly decrease the water supply in certain areas, including the area around Lake Turkana. As a consequence, there will be further competition over scarce resources for the 200,000–300,000 indigenous peoples who live around the lake (Human Rights Watch 2012a: p. 10). The dam also threatens the food security and the ecological system of this area. Through the alteration of the Oma River's flood cycle and the water levels in Lake Turkina the local economies that support more than half a million people will be harshly affected (International Rivers 2012). The impoverishment of the wetland area through the altering of the River and the Lake levels will impact negatively on the ecosystems of Turkana and Lower Omo including the lake's fisheries which "are the main source of protein for local people (dried fish are also sold, and are a major source of income). Large mammal populations will lose habitat, food sources and migration corridors" (Greste 2009: p. 4). As noted by the African Union Development Bank hydrology study (International Rivers 2011: p. 2), "the water volume to fill Gibe III reservoir would deprive the lake of

85% of its normal annual inflow in one year . . . The potential impact on the lake is significant. The filling of the dam has the potential to dry up the most productive fishing area of the lake."

The World Bank is supporting other mass hydropower projects including the Inga 3 Dam project on the Congo River—a $12 billion investment and two other multi-billion-dollar projects on the Zambezi River. These projects, as with others in the past, will not benefit the local communities, but rather will be the primary source of electricity for the surrounding mining companies and the upper-class population (Bosshard 2013).

Water availability projects

The World Bank's International Finance Corporation (2013) has asserted that: "Water is a cross-cutting resource that is critical for human survival and water availability and access are at the top of the global development agenda" (p. 1). However, its support of the forced or coerced privatization of water is instead leading to increased costs, less availability and social harm for the most vulnerable populations. The large multinational corporations pushing for the expansion of privatization are the principal beneficiaries of this endeavor. The World Bank has privileged profits for corporations within the "water industry" over projects that would produce long-term solutions for water-related problems (Common Dreams 2012: p. 2).

A recent report by Corporate Accountability International (2012: p. 11) states that "thirty-four percent of all private water contracts market wide entered between 2000 and 2010 have failed or are in distress—four times the failure rates of comparable infrastructure projects in the electric and transportation sectors." Given the problems of early privatization projects during the 1990s, the World Bank reformatted the privatized model from that of corporations owning and operating water utilities to the privatization of outsourcing water distribution operations. Currently, the Bank is set to spend billions on water privatization effort with the Bank's private-sector arm increasing investments to $1 billion each year as of 2013 (see Appendix C for an overview of current projects approved and committed to). Additionally, many of the Bank's loans continue to require conversion of public water systems to privatized or semi-privatized, known as public-private partnership, as a condition for general loans. This new model is meant to increase the profits of private companies by "encouraging" their participation in municipal/state services, keeping the risk and responsibility away from corporations by making the public sector responsible for it.

Privatization projects relating to the availability of water have escalated, to the detriment of expanding on the basic human right to have access to water. For example, in numerous states in India, public-private partnerships for water projects are being widely implemented. The Bank and its International Finance Corporation arm are also sponsoring the privatization of water sectors in several other countries in Asia and Africa (see Appendix C). Under the International Finance Corporation's *Safe Water for Africa* program in partnership with Coca-Cola, Diago and Water Health International, it is promoting privatized provision of water in villages across Ghana and elsewhere (Alhassan 2011). In October 2011, the International Finance Corporation announced a new partner venture with Nestlé, Coca-Cola and Veolia, the 2013 Water Resources Group Phase 2 to "transform the water sector." It is currently working with the governments of Mexico and Jordan and Karnataka (India) on such projects. However, these projects generally do not lead to the improvement of water-related services. Rather, they principally produce profits for private corporations.

"Intervention" centers

In a World Bank–funded project in Vietnam involving government detention centers for individuals dependent on drugs, scores of human rights abuses were committed (Human Rights Watch 2012b). These abuses—committed in the name of rehabilitation—included arbitrary detention, forced labor, torture, and other forms of ill treatment in 14 detention centers. Between 2000 and 2010, over 309,000 people passed through the centers where they were forced to provide manual labor and lived in conditions violating basic rights. Former detainees told Human Rights Watch that they had been beaten with "wooden truncheons, shocked with electrical batons, and deprived of food and water" (Human Rights Watch 2012b: p. 9). Government regulations mandate that labor therapy (lao dong tri lieu) be a central component of drug rehabilitation and is not optional. If detainees refuse to work, they are punished. All detainees are supposed to have the right to receive treatment. In practice, however, treatment has not been given due to either lack of services or outright refusal to provide it. Support centers for HIV and other health services have instead had the perverse effect of facilitating continued detention.

The World Bank supported the "intervention" center program, with $35 million for health care programs and $1.5 million through 2005–2012 for services including an HIV and health care screening process and treatment. When the World Bank was alerted to and provided with evidence of the human rights violations occurring within these programs, the response was negligible at best. It stated that the part of the project that received direct funds had been completed and therefore their obligations and responsibility had ended (Human Rights Watch 2013).

Conclusion

This chapter reviewed some recent cases of crimes of globalization with the role of the international financial institutions highlighted. While criticisms of the policies and practices of international financial institutions date back to late 1980s and earlier, these current cases document that crimes of globalization are ongoing. They are a core byproduct of the neo-liberal agenda masked as "development." Crimes of globalization are ultimately about ongoing symbiotic relationships and processes involving a range of entities based in both sponsoring Western and global North countries and the global South countries. These entities include the international financial institutions, their sponsoring states (especially the United States), multinational corporations and businesses, and corrupt elite political and business leaders in many of the global South states. In a truly sophisticated accounting of crimes of globalization, the specific *actions* of international financial institutions development officers and others, and specific sponsored *projects* and specific *events* that arise out of this (e.g., violent suppression of anti-dam protests, open-pit mining protests, pipeline protests) are manifestations of structural, systemic crimes. However, there may well be a hypothetical inverse relationship between the most sophisticated conception of such crime and the most effective conception, relative to public awareness and civil society mobilization against such crime.

4

TOWARDS AN INTEGRATED THEORY OF CRIMES OF GLOBALIZATION

The terms "mainstream" and "orthodox criminology"—sometimes "modern criminology"—refer to the dominant orientation of most contemporary criminologists. Mainstream criminology is principally positivistic (or scientific) in orientation. A quantitative dimension is common to such work. The positivistic orientation of mainstream criminology has been criticized on many grounds (Young 2011). In one view, a positivistic criminology is inherently biased to focus on those forms of crime and its control that lend themselves most easily to measurement: that is, conventional crime and its control.

We endorse the view—derived from a sociology of knowledge approach—that the dominant theories, methods and substantive concerns of criminology as a field of study, at any given point in time, are a function of such factors as the student experiences, institutional affiliations, professional networks, graduate student pools of particular criminologists, as well as the social and political climate in any given period (Hauhart 2012; Savelsberg and Flood 2004). All of these factors surely have contributed to the almost total neglect of crimes of globalization by criminologists to date, with a few exceptions. But it is our conviction, as we expressed earlier, that a confluence of conditions may well transform this circumstance. We obviously hope that this book contributes to a measurable increase in criminological attention to crimes of globalization.

Little attention has been given to the value of traditional criminological theories for addressing crimes of globalization. While many such theories contribute significantly to our understanding of conventional criminal activities and juvenile delinquency, as independent theories they have serious shortcomings (Agnew 2011; Rothe 2009). Criminological inquiry has principally produced theories addressing one specific level of analysis (e.g., individual, interactional, organizational, or structural). Utilizing theories that explain only the individual level processes or even that of organizations or the broader structure is bound to overlook the interdependent nature of social reality. More often than not, the underlying assumptions of these theories are left unaddressed, regardless of their impact on theory generation. Perhaps more importantly, there remains a divide within criminology on what theory is and what it should accomplish (Agnew 2011). Any initiatives at explanation of crimes of globalization should begin with a sense of humility and with acknowledgment that the world we live in is endlessly complex, with countless different variables interacting on multiple different levels. Accordingly, full-fledged explanation and prediction is tremendously difficult. Prior to exploring the value of criminological theory for crimes of globalization, a brief discussion is in order to clarify the purpose of theory and what it is meant to accomplish, followed by an overview of theoretical integration.

Theory: its purpose and form

Theory can be thought of as a set of logically related concepts that can explain a phenomenon. An alternative view is that theory is a set of logically related postulates-propositions-hypotheses that can be empirically tested and falsified and that is capable of being predictive. The latter view reflects a scientific and positivistic interpretation of theory, which holds that without the ability to empirically and statistically test a theory and subject it to possible falsification, it has no validity or scientific value. Yet as Bernard (1990: p. 327) argued, falsification of criminological theories failed insofar as "no theoretical approach to crime has ever been falsified in the history of criminology." Theory that is "testable"— generally understood by mainstream criminologists as quantifiably tested by a sophisticated statistical program—has come to dominate the field: making it falsifiable and parsimonious. However, this assumes a level of simplicity about the human condition and for crimes of globalization provides a minimalistic approach to addressing the intertwinement of a host of factors that explain such crime. Bureaucratic organizations such as international financial institutions, and their personnel, cannot be understood in terms of scientific theories that are used to explain natural and physical phenomena. Parsimonious, simplistic theories and positivist methodologies are unable to capture the complexities of the environment and the circumstances within which crimes of globalization occur. They tend to reduce complex human and social phenomena to a few measurable variables to establish causal relationships. A valid theoretical model for crimes of globalization must take into account the complexities of the global economic system and the intertwinement of factors from the structural to the interactional the individualistic level. The objective here is to produce a theoretical framework with broad explanatory validity, rather than a "falsifiable" or "testable" theory. As Karl Popper (1959) argued, the truth or soundness of a proposition is not uniformly dependent upon falsification by scientific methods.

Criminological theories apply to different levels of analysis. Each of these can be thought of as operating along a continuum from the micro to the macro level. The distinction between these various levels of analysis is relevant to the types of crimes being analyzed as well as the theoretical model that can be applied. For example, a theoretical approach that explains individual level behavior may have limited explanatory power. Theories that explain street crime, for example, will differ from those that attempt to explain organizational crimes such as corporate crime, state crime or crimes of globalization. And a sophisticated understanding of crimes of globalization requires integration of several different levels of analysis. But it does not follow from this that traditional criminological theories have no value for the project of understanding crimes of globalization. In the discussion that follows we identify dimensions of these traditional theories that have some relevance for this project. Ultimately dimensions of these theories need to be incorporated into an integrated, multi-level theory of crimes of globalization.

Theory integration

Theory integration can take several forms: it can be specific or general (Cullen and Agnew 2003), propositional or conceptual (Liska *et al.* 1989), static or dynamic (Barak 1997). It can combine two or more existing theories, concepts, and propositions into one more comprehensive model (Barak 1997; Farnworth 1989). These theories, concepts and propositions may be closely related or may be competing models. There is also side-by-side integration, which involves integrating partial theories to explain a phenomenon, or end-to-end integration that entails shuffling variables from one theory to another, making the dependent variable the independent variable and vice versa. An up-and-down integration is the development of a "general" theory that includes multiple propositions from specific theories. Integration can combine single levels or multiple levels; it can be intra-disciplinary or inter-disciplinary. Integrated macro-micro theories "focus on both the individual and the structure plus on some kind of interaction between the two" (Barak 1997: p. 198). As Wellford (1989) notes, due to the complexity of human behavior and the multi-"causal" factors identified in existing criminological research, a multi-level, multi-disciplinary integration is necessary. This is perhaps even more pertinent to an integrated theory for crimes of globalization as "[t]his type of integration places causal significance on both large-scale social forces and individual-level adaptations that result in criminal events" (Roundtree *et al.* 1994: p. 388). The latter approach is taken here for an integrated theory of crimes of globalization.

An integrated theory of crimes of globalization

Matthew Robinson (2004) has identified the principal dimensions or levels that should be part of an integrated theory of crime as: cell (e.g., genes); organ (e.g., a brain injury); organism (e.g., self-control, strain);

group (e.g., social learning, differential association); community (e.g., social control, efficacy, network); organization (e.g., labeling, social disorganization); and society (e.g., anomie). One can add to this listing—which is in any case not necessarily exhaustive—global context (e.g., systems, neo-liberal policies). Integrated theories have also been applied to explain organizational offending (Vaughan 1982), including corporate crime (Kramer and Michalowski 1990; Tombs and Whyte 2007), and state-corporate crime and state crime (Kauzlarich and Kramer 1998). The latter group of integrated theories that address organizational crimes are drawn from and expanded on here to help illuminate international financial institutions' actions along with two additional proposed perspectives: Foucauldian and system criminality. One of the authors—independently and with colleagues—has built explicitly on the theoretical framework produced by Kauzlarich and Kramer (1998) in relation to state-corporate crime, which itself built on earlier work by Kramer and Michalowski (1990) to present an integrated model of offending that explored motivation, opportunities, controls and constraints at four levels of analysis (interactional, organizational, state/ structural, and international) (Rothe and Mullins 2008; Rothe and Ross 2010; Rothe 2006, 2009). In doing so, the integrated framework combines insights and core concepts from criminological theories and other disciplines to explain the multiple levels at play within each specific case.

For example, from the criminological literature, social learning (e.g., differential association), strain, rational choice, routine activities, techniques of neutralization, and anomie theories can address specific components of interactional and organizational offending.

Each of these is discussed more fully in the following paragraphs.

Rational choice theory

Rational choice models are typically associated with the classical school of criminological thought. Cornish and Clarke (1986) developed one version of rational choice theory. This theory assumes that offenders act after a rational decision-making process that includes (1) the initial choice to become involved, and then (2) the decision whether to commit a criminal act. The key differentiation to the classical school of

---

International Level

Motivations—Political and economic interests, resources, ideologies.

Opportunities—International relations, economic/military supremacy, complementary legal systems.

Constraints/Controls—International reactions, political pressure, public opinion, social movements, NGOs, Oversight and economic institutions, international law and/or sanctions.

State Level (Macro)

Motivations—Structural transformations, economic pressure or goals, political goals, ethnogenses.

Opportunity—Availability of illegal means, control of information, propaganda, ideology/nationalism, military capabilities.

Constraints/Controls—Political pressure, media scrutiny, public opinion, social movements, rebellion, legal sanctions, domestic law.

Organizational Level (Meso)

Motivations—Organizational culture and goals, authoritarian pressure, reward structures.

Opportunities—Communications structures, means availability, role specialization.

Constraints/Controls—Internal oversight, authority/command structures, codes of conduct.

Interactional Level (Micro)

Motivations—Strain, socialization, individual goals, ideologies, and traits, definition of the situation, perceived objectives/reality, normalization of deviance, group think, obedience to authority.

Opportunity—Diffusion of responsibilities, perceived illegal means.

Constraints/Controls—Personal morality/ethical code, informal social controls, perceived legitimacy of law and its applications.

FIGURE 4.1 An integrated theory of crime

thought is the inclusion of bounded rationality. Simply stated, bounded rationality views the decision-making process as influenced by incomplete or inaccurate information. This is due to social factors and individual estimates of perceived costs and benefits (Rothe 2009). In relation to crimes of globalization, bounded rationality can be applied at the individual level within the context of a rational bureaucratic organization.

Structural Criminological Theories

e.g., Political Economy; Neo-realism; Anomie; System Criminality; Foucault—regimes of truth and power; and Realpolitik

Organizational Criminological Theories

Organizational Theory—culture, ideology, standard operating procedures, internal pressures, legitimacy, reward structures, diffusion of responsibilities; Strain; Routine Activities; and Techniques of Neutralization

Interactional Criminological Theories

Strain; Rational Choice theory; Learning theory

FIGURE 4.2 Towards theory generation

As will be discussed below, organizations influence individual decision-making due to the information provided to individual actors, influencing in turn the estimates of the perceived costs and benefits of their action.

Cohen and Felson (1979) further developed the rational choice theory to include choice constrained by opportunity. The elements of routine activities include a motivated offender (a given), suitable targets (opportunity), and capable guardians (operationality of control). This follows Cornish and Clarke's concept of bounded rationality but illuminates the situational factors. While rational choice theory is often viewed as a theory of victimization, Cohen and Felson provided three key catalysts that are indeed relevant to all crime, including crimes of the state and other violations of international criminal law. If we accept that bounded rationality can be a factor of individual decision-making within an organizational setting, routine activities theory then highlights the importance of recognizing the need for opportunity for a crime to occur and for a lack of control to constrain or block the actor's decision to act at that specific time. In other words, the organizations (international financial institutions) and the actors within them must have the opportunity to pursue the policies that result in crimes of globalization. As will be discussed in the next chapter, the lack of guardian and control does provide carte blanche power to pursue opportunities that have long been criticized for doing more harm than good.

Techniques of neutralization

Techniques of neutralization also play a role in crime-related decision-making. Sykes and Matza (1957) presented concepts of neutralization and justification that include (1) denial of responsibility, (2) denial of injury, (3) denial of victim, (4) condemnation of the condemner, and (5) appeal to higher authority. These techniques can best be understood in terms of the simple process of rationalizing one's own behavior, whether in response to cognitive dissonance, as a precondition to acting, or other factors; it is a process of rationalization. Such processes can be prior to an act, aiding a cost-benefit analysis, or post-action to minimize a person's behaviors. This model can aid in our understanding of the discourse within the organizational setting, negating the impact of decision-making and subsequent policies. International financial institutions have denied responsibility for their funded projects and subsequent victimization to the local people or environment (e.g., Pak Mun Dam); they condemn the condemners in the case of anti-globalization protests.

Learning theories

Learning theories share certain assumptions of human nature and their relation to the social environment within which they exist. The assumption here is that individuals are shaped, and can be reshaped, by specific environments and/or conditions. The process of normal learning can generate criminal behavior as well as conforming behavior. The key to these theories is the process of learning and the subsequent content of what is learned. Edwin H. Sutherland (1949) is the most well-known criminologist associated with learning theories, and is of course the founder of the criminology of white collar crime. As noted by Sutherland (1949: p. 300), "Any person can be trained to adopt and follow a pattern of criminal behavior." Through the processes of socialization, individuals learn how to define their environment, favorable or unfavorable attitudes, and specific behaviors. This is important within the organizational setting. Consider your own employment and how, while you are there, you are trained to follow a specific pattern of behavior acceptable to your employer. You learn the standard operating procedures as well as those little shortcuts that employees take to increase their productivity or decrease their workload. You also learn to define, as favorable or unfavorable, specific attitudes and behaviors within the confines of your daily job activities. This is no different for employees of international financial institutions where they learn, through socialization, what is defined as favorable or unfavorable decisions and actions. These are guided by the larger organizational culture and ideology (i.e., neo-liberalism).

Anomie theory

The concept of anomie is related in many ways to the political economy, yet is also distinct in that cultural goals of organizations need not be tied to economic goal attainment. Émile Durkheim's (1897) classic discussion of anomie argues that it reflects the normlessness associated with rapidly changing societies, wherein traditional norms no longer constrain individuals and new norms are adopted. However, confusion arising out of conflicts between traditional and emerging norms encourages unregulated aspirations and egoism. The concept of chronic economic anomie with resulting long-term diminution of social regulation is relevant to many crimes of the powerful, including corporate, state-corporate, state crime, and crimes of globalization (see Rothe and Ross 2010). In a Mertonian sense, anomie is the result of a high emphasis on corporate (international financial institutions) goals with low emphasis placed on institutionalized norms to achieve these goals. The social structure has an inherent contradiction between the expected aspirations (cultural goals) and obtainable legitimate means to achieve these culturally emphasized goals. Combining these definitions, anomie can be understood as a condition of the larger environment wherein a great emphasis is placed on the goals of the international financial institutions, but there is a lack of regulation and standardized norms that guide the goal achievement (internally and externally). As will be discussed in the following chapter, international financial institutions operate without external and often internal regulation. Consequently, anomic conditions are intensified.

Merton's (1938) classic structure-strain theory is also of relevance. According to Merton, strain occurs when attempts to achieve goals and expectations are unattainable, either due to blocked goals or means. Individuals may then respond in several ways to this strain: conformity, innovation, ritualism, and rebellion. For actors within the organizational setting of international financial institutions, such strain can occur due to pressure to lend policies that put priorities in approving loans that should be rejected or by external pressure exerted by multi-national corporations for specific projects to be approved, regardless of the difficulties presented to approve a policy or loan by the potential receiving state. In the previous example, where the International Monetary Fund agreed to a loan for $4.8 billion to Egypt, the discussions and pressure to approve the loan began in November of the previous year, yet the project was postponed due to mass protests by Egyptian workers and unemployed young people. The International Monetary Fund bureaucrats are rewarded for obtaining fast approvals, which can cause strain when quotas are not met.

Organizational theory

Likewise, sociological organizational analysis plays an important explanatory role (e.g., organizational culture, sub-units, role specialization, and task segregation, reward structures, and goal attainment). Here, the importance of choice and bounded-rationality are widely accepted as parts of organizational analysis given their bureaucratic structure. Situated action—that is, the impact of an environment affects individuals' decision-making and choices—is at the heart of organizational theories. Simply put, a good person can be brought to "evil" action within certain situations and environments. There is the recognition that we all become socialized into specific organizational contexts in which we find ourselves. Through "differential association" we learn the expected behaviors and the organizations goals and missions. As MacKenzie (2006: p. 167) notes, once international financial institutions were created, they developed their own "internal cultures, discourses, rationalizations and futures." This includes the discourse that enables individual actors to neutralize and rationalize their actions and policies (e.g., condemning the condemner, denial of victims or harm). These cultural goals can also lead to individual strain when the broader goals are blocked and/or without a clear set of means to achieve them. As anomie theory suggests, any organization that operates without any external (and internal) controls generates structures of increasing opportunity to commit crime. When an unrestricted "appetite" for profit and fulfillment of an ideology (neo-liberalism) is left unconstrained, a criminogenic organizational environment emerges. Within such a criminogenic environment, enough is never enough. Once an organizational culture exists, it becomes institutionalized, making it far more difficult to alter short of a major institutional transformation. As organizational theorists point out, organizational cultures and goals remain intact even as employees are replaced. However, organizations are neither a monolithic entity nor do they operate within a vacuum. This is especially the case for international financial institutions, as they operate within a global context, being affected by and affecting states and corporations. The approach outlined here recognizes agency at the interactional level, while simultaneously noting the impact of organizational culture and the broader structure on the individual level of decision-making.

System criminality theory

We suggest that the concept of system criminality can further aid our understanding of crimes of globalization. System criminality has been conceptualized as crimes that are committed by individual actors and organizations that constitute a complex whole with varying levels of participation (Nollkaemper and Van Der Wilt 2009). This emphasizes the role of the system within which individual actions result in a crime. The term has also been used to describe the systematic means through which a crime is carried out. Crimes of globalization are systemic in nature, and often involve elements of collective responsibility. International financial institutions on both the individual and the organizational level carry out their crimes in cooperation with state and

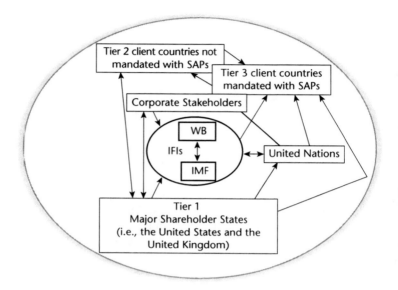

FIGURE 4.3 The global system: system criminality

corporate entities. The concept of system criminality recognizes the whole of relationships within which various actors' actions occur along a continuum of involvement (Rothe and Collins 2011). The meaningfulness of this concept is that it provides a tool through which one can analyze the complex web of connections between and amongst various entities (i.e., transnational corporations, international organizations, states, and international financial institutions).

Figure 4.3 offers an illustration of the totality of the system within which crimes of globalization occur. At the center are the international financial institutions which are impacted by the major stakeholders, states and their corporate entities that have vested interests. Likewise, the United Nations is affected by and impacts on the international financial institutions. What we call Tier 1 (Major shareholder states—i.e., the United States and the United Kingdom) impacts on the UN as well as Tier 2 (client countries not mandated with SAPs) and Tier 3 (client states mandated with SAPs) (i.e., Senegal, Uganda, Egypt, etc.), primarily this category includes the majority of the global South countries. At the core, the international financial institutions exert immense influence and impact on the Tier 2 and Tier 3 countries. Consequentially, to examine the international financial institution's harms or crimes of globalization (including crimes of omission), one must be cognizant of and analyze the totality of relations that constitute the system. The decision-making at the organizational level of the international financial institutions does not occur within a vacuum. The influence of other entities identified here must be taken into account.

Unlike organizational theories, system criminality is not bound by the confines of a particular organization or its immediate environment (Vaughan 2002). Similarly, system criminality, as we define it, expands beyond network theories that deal with individual actors, their interactions and how the structure of ties affects relationships, to the collectivities of a broader system (Freeman 2004; Moody and White 2003). Recognizing the totality of the globalized system also negates the compartmentalizing of actors, organizations, and policies. If the focus is on atomistic organizations or individuals, we would be limiting our concerns and responses to "small cogs in larger systems" (Nollkaemper 2009: p. 2).

A Foucauldian perspective and "regimes of truth"

Foucault has been influential in the critical assessment of relations between power and truth. For Foucault, power is everywhere, not solely a coercive force. Mechanisms of power—means in which it is dispersed—produce "knowledge" that reinforces the exercise of that power. This is done through several means, including discourse. Truth is a construct of the political and economic forces that hold the majority of power within and external to a society. For Foucault (1977: p. 2): "'Truth' is linked in a circular relation with systems of power which produce and sustain it, and to effects of power which it induces and which extend it: a 'regime' of truth."

From our perspective, crimes of globalization are inherently situated in and reify existing relations of power. As such, Foucault's assessment of power, discourse, and regimes of truth are useful for explaining the harms generated by international financial institutions and can be usefully applied to crimes of globalization (Rothe 2010a,b). From a Foucauldian standpoint, international financial institutions can be said to be a site where capitalistic hegemonic power is exercised (Rothe 2010a,b; Welch 2008). According to Foucault (1977), power extends beyond states' apparatuses, as do politics. Soft power provides the realm wherein political persuasion could be used to advance the "virtues" of neo-liberalism (Ferguson 2005). For example, the Foucauldian notions of "truth" and a "regime of truth" undergirds the concept of "development." The idea of discourse includes a statement of how "development" is defined, followed by the rules guiding the ways it is discussed, and how this then frames the authority of "truth" about the subject (development) (Foucault 1980). The "regime of truth" then guides the practice within the institution for dealing with the subject (development) that is embedded in a system primarily dominated by state and corporate interests (Rothe 2010a,b).

With Foucault, it is not the statement of "truth" that decides about the functionality, acceptance and/or effectiveness of definitorial powers, it is the "material reality" of a societal "regime of truth," in this case the international financial community (Foucault 1980: p. 131). This "material reality" can be said to be represented by the interactions of international players (Ewald 2008): in particular, the system, as described above, involved within the global finance/banking processes. This "regime of truth" then serves to undergird the operational practice of international financial institutions. It also serves as the political discourse designed to legitimate policies of international financial institutions. Figure 4.4 provides a visual schematic of this process.

Further, this truth becomes understood as what Gramsci referred to as "common sense" or as Giambattista Vico (1948: p. 63) stated as "judgment without reflection." This then comes to be seen as a generalized way of thinking that becomes dominant in a certain era, reflecting not only what is to be known but also what should and is to be done in the economic sphere. Consequentially, while the potential for "genuine debate has to be informed at some level by knowledge of the social origins of public problems," this is removed when such discourse does not allow for additional "truths" (Rosenfeld 2002: p. 5).

FIGURE 4.4 A Foucauldian perspective

We are suggesting that the ideology of neo-liberalism and market fundamentalism is framed as development (hegemonic discourse framing the issue). As was noted earlier, a genuine belief in the neo-liberal policies that guide mandated restructuring policies exists. This ideology serves to undergird the ways in which development is portrayed, discussed and understood. This includes terms such as economic stability and poverty reduction. This becomes the "truth." The truth is embedded within the broader interests of protecting corporate and state capital accumulation (neo-liberal ideology) and becomes "common sense," leaving no room for critique of or alternatives to the proposed solutions. This "truth" reifies the overarching "regime of truth" which is sustaining and, in a dialectic sense, reinforcing the status quo at the benefit of major stakeholders' interests. In other words, the regime of truth supports the status quo, appears as common sense and as if consensually accepted. Subsequent measures of implementing policy dictated by this "truth" become institutionalized within the organizational culture. For example, the International Monetary Fund states that global economic health and an end to poverty can only happen through major structural adjustments (now often referred to as Poverty Reduction Strategy Papers under the Heavily Indebted Poor Countries Initiative) (HIPC): "The IMF works to foster global growth and economic stability. It provides policy advice and financing to members in economic difficulties and also works with developing nations to help them achieve macroeconomic stability and reduce poverty" (International Monetary Fund 2013b: p. 1). The means to achieve this "truth" is through policies that have become accepted as common sense: structural adjustments. As the former Chief Economist of the World Bank Joseph Stiglitz (2002: p. 12) states:

> Founded on the belief that there is a need for international pressure on countries to have more expansionary economic policies—such as increasing expenditures, reducing taxes, lowering interest rates to stimulate the economy—today the IMF typically provides funds only if countries engage in policies like cutting deficits, raising taxes, or raising interest rates that lead to a contraction of the economy.

Once institutionalized, it becomes difficult to alter these belief systems/truths, given a highly complex bureaucratic structure, other than in the case of a major institutional shake-up. In light of the absence of significant controls over the policies and practices of international financial institutions, the entrenched belief system will continue to drive these policies and practices.

Political economy theories

Political economy models have been used to explain the driving forces at the state and international levels, in terms of motivation. The importance of the economy cannot be overstated in the context of addressing crimes of globalization. The earliest version of political economy theory emphasized the relation between the economic system of production with the government and law. This was later revised and expanded to include the international political economy (and international relations). The emphasis here, while broadened, remains on the relations between economic systems and politics within a country and between countries (Underhill 2000). Specifically, the concern is with the ways political forces, including those of international financial institutions, shape broader systems through economic interactions and how the economy interacts with these political structures (international financial institutions in the case at hand) (Oatley 2009). The global political economy is drawn on to demonstrate the economic pressures impacting states, transnational or multinational organizational crimes and crimes of globalization (see Friedrichs and Friedrichs 2002). Consider the recent (2013) economic and political situation in Egypt following the Arab Spring where social inequality continues to be a huge problem (Abdou and Zaazou 2013). Under immense pressure from elites to improve the country's economy President Mohamed Morsi announced an agreement with the International Monetary Fund for a $4.8 billion loan, opening markets further to Western states. After the ousting of Morsi in 2013, Egypt continued to pursue the loan agreement with the International Monetary Fund. Given the internal unrest and current economic conditions, however, austerity measures demanded by the IMF will have devastating social, political, and economic consequences. After all, the massive protests in June, 2013, that led to President Morsi being forced out of office were driven in part by rising anger over economic conditions in Egypt (Ersado 2012).

Summary

The integration of criminological theories outlined in this chapter allows us to address the broader system, the organizational context, and actors involved in crimes of globalization. Figure 4.5 attempts to visually display the proposed integrated theoretical framework.

We have here situated the actors, organizations, and theoretical perspectives within the broader systems within which crimes of

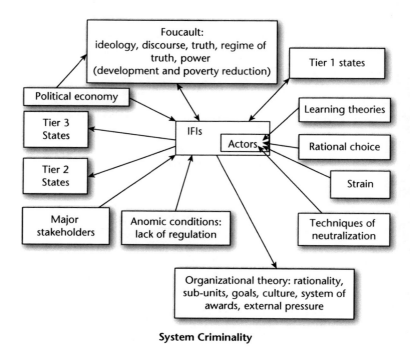

System Criminality

FIGURE 4.5 Towards an integrated theory of crimes of globalization

globalization occur. While international financial institutions remain in the center, they are impacted by and impact on the Foucauldian concepts of truth, regimes of truth and discourses. Anomie and political economy perspectives come into play in relation to the international financial institutions. Organizational theories aid our understanding of the decision-making of the organization and the processes within them, including the impact of the organizational culture on individual actors within the organization. Social learning theory, strain theory, techniques of neutralization, and rational choice come into play in relation to individual actors within the organizational settings of the international financial institutions. The following section attempts to elucidate the relevance of the integrated framework.

Theoretical relevance: the policies and practices of the international financial institutions

> "When I use a word," Humpty Dumpty said, in a rather scornful tone, "it means what I choose it to mean. Neither more nor less."
>
> "The question is," said Alice, "whether you can make words mean so many different things."
>
> "The questions is," said Humpty Dumpty, "who is to be master. That is all."
>
> (Lewis Carroll, *Through the Looking-Glass*)

International financial institutions have stated a commitment to suppressing corruption associated with international aid within debtor states. The realization of the need to address corruption is based on the belief that it hinders external investment and "retards economic growth." However, in many situations the international financial institutions are directly or indirectly involved in facilitating corruption on a vast scale. This can include financing projects that the international financial institutions know are embedded in a corrupt system, through allowing loan money to be misappropriated, or knowingly contracting corrupt corporations to carry out international financial institutions' projects. For example, during the late 1990s, twenty-one Western power companies were investigated for corruption, alleged kickbacks, and over-pricing. While the companies filed statements denying corruption, six of the twenty-one companies later confessed to corrupt activities (Hawley 2000). The World Bank initially sent in a team of investigators, yet the International Monetary Fund "went so far as to make a new package of loans at the end of 1998 conditional on the Pakistan government's dropping the charges against the companies" (Hawley 2000: p. 15). Moreover, in conflict-ridden regions, promotion of privatization and/or mega-infrastructure projects facilitate conditions that are already heavily embedded with high levels of corruption, violence, and, more often than not, massive violations of human rights. Corruption has also been linked with the over-focus of international financial institutions on debt repayment, debt status, and a country's levels of exports. The question we need to ask ourselves is why that is happening given the stated commitment of the international financial institutions to "ending" corruption.

The ideology behind the "truth" and "regime of truth" is the deep-seated belief in neo-liberalism and free trade as "the route to development" (MacKenzie 2006: p. 172). This is situated within the broader system (system criminality) of actors (e.g., states and multi-national corporations). Additionally, the broader ideology or regime of truth (development) that is reinforced by the international political economy cannot be ignored in terms of motivating forces (see Figure 4.5). We suggest that realpolitik—a political ideology that prioritizes the economic, military, and political interests of states above moral and ethical obligations—and the international political economy are major catalysts influencing international financial institutions' interests and investments, including those that facilitate corruption.

The role and relationships of the international financial institutions, stakeholders (including corporations and their lobbyists and Western states), and client states are relevant to this type of crime of globalization. The World Bank and the International Monetary Fund operate under the marked political influence of certain countries, the holders of the majority votes. The United States has the most votes and is the single most dominant country. Realpolitik plays a role in motivating international financial institutions to extend loans and aid to highly corrupt regimes. Major donors pressure the institutions to support country B as country A has a vested economic, political, or military interest in that country. The hugely corrupt Suharto regime in Indonesia is just one example of a country long-supported on this basis. Given the mutual interdependence of the major powers and the international financial institutions, such political pressure can easily translate into decision-making not in the interest of ending corruption.

The so-called G8 countries (Canada, France, Germany, Italy, Japan, Russia, the United Kingdom, and the United States) place a high priority on advancing the interest of private companies within their borders. This priority influences the Structural Adjustment Policies (SAPs) of the international financial institutions. As previously pointed out, "[p]olitics has always influenced the advice offered by the IMF and World Bank . . . World Bank projects are sometimes covertly shaped by pre-existing agreements for contracts between large companies backed by powerful governments and borrowers" (Woods 2006: p. 5). Nearly one-half of the monies the World Bank lends is dispersed directly to corporations through its "international competitive bidding," with the majority going to companies based within the major developed countries. An April 2009 report, "Corporate Misgovernance at the World Bank," confirms this as it notes that "serving on the board of directors at the International Bank for Reconstruction and Development (IBRD) doubles funding opportunities for the board members' home countries by about $60 million" (Kaja and Werker 2009: p. 2). A recent evaluation by the Internal Evaluation Office (2012) of the International Monetary Fund stated that the political priorities of the fund's major members can influence what is ostensibly objective analysis by an apolitical organization. The report included criticism that IMF aid to Europe to address the financial crisis was more generous than programs for Asia and Latin America. The report stated that IMF staff began research on China's accumulation of foreign reserves in "response to frustration" among "influential shareholders" that China was not allowing its exchange rate to fluctuate more freely (Schneider 2012: p. 2). States pressure international financial institutions to approve loans for specific contractors and/ or regimes that are questionable, have negative track records, or would otherwise not qualify—due to their own self-interests (economic, military, and political), whether that be for their ally or against their foe (economic strangulation). As noted by MacKenzie (2006: p. 168):

> [T]he relationship between favorable outcomes for financiers and corporations in developed nations is not a case of simple string pulling in respect of puppet institutions. There is some level of influence that may be characterized as fairly direct: corporate lobbying, the bare threats and other less obvious coercive political tactics employed by developed nations in negotiations, and at root the power of veto given to the U.S. in relation to the IMF and the World Bank. International financial institutions also operate in an anomic environment.

For example, there are no external controls or institutions that provide any regulation of international financial institutions. Consequentially, there is some confusion on which norms and rules apply. This is in line with Durkheim's notion of anomie. If we consider anomie in Merton's terms, international financial institutions' aspirations and goals remain unlimited and without legitimate means to attain them. International relations, power, and the practice of realpolitik at the structural level filters down to the organizational and interactional level, creating a culture wherein donor desires, political interests, and economic profits take primacy over any professed claims to aid developing countries or to end corruption in these countries. Ultimately, then, decision-making with the international financial institutions is hugely influenced by corporate lobbyists, major funding donors and the interests of dominant states.

Enhancing profit remains a core objective for the major "donors" and their transnational corporations, as well as for the international financial institutions. Accordingly, the lending practices of the international financial institutions are heavily oriented toward the realization of this goal.

The culture of an organization strongly influences individual-level decision-making and organizational policies. This is a core tenet of organizational theory. In line with such theory the cultural values and goals of an organization remain intact as executives and employees come and go. Actors within an organization adapt to the culture, the routines and practices of the organization through a learning process. This is a core tenet of differential association theory.

International financial institutions are highly bureaucratic organizations, where diffusion of responsibility, pressure to lend, and reward structures largely determine individual decision-making. As a consequence, loans benefitting corrupt political regimes and corporations get approved. Corruption is tolerated when it protects or promotes organizational goals (Green and Ward 2004). Goals of development coupled with the promotion of profit fosters corruption. The "pressure to lend" culture of the World Bank and the International Monetary Fund—whose officers are rewarded for getting loans out—inevitably leads to highly questionable or basically harmful loans (Shah 2008; Bretton Woods Project 2006). The underlying incentive structures encourage "success" with large, costly projects. International financial institutions are structured to reward their loan officials for technical proficiency rather than for concerning themselves with the perspectives and the needs of the people of developing countries (Bradlow 1996: p. 75). The threat of not succeeding or losing one's job due to non-approval of projects contributes to individual strain for loan officials. Such strain translates to the organizational level where a "culture of approval" and a reward structure is reified into decisions at odds with the protection of human rights or the doctrine of curtailing corruption. Such decisions can then be neutralized by invoking the discourse of "aid," "development," and the reduction of poverty. The "regime of truth," which supports the interests of the powerful in the Western and global North, works against the interest of the people of the global South countries and is reinforced by the same policies.

In sum, the international financial institutions promote campaigns to combat corruption in global South countries. But the goals of these campaigns are largely if not wholly subordinated to realizing other objectives of the international financial institutions' loan officials and their sponsors. A range of factors that we have discussed come together to produce a criminogenic environment where crimes of globalization can flourish.

Conclusion

This chapter has set forth some key dimensions of an integrated theory of crimes of globalization. Many challenges arise in the formulation of any such theory. The need for refinements to the integrated theory outlined here is clear. Nonetheless, we hope that we have laid a foundation for an integrated theory that contributes to explaining and understanding crimes of globalization. Such an integrated theory does not lend itself readily to empirical verification. We have noted earlier the attraction for many criminologists of uni-dimensional theories that can be easily tested. But it is our position that crimes of globalization are highly complex and their understanding requires the adoption of a multi-dimensional, integrated theoretical model.

5

CRIMES OF GLOBALIZATION AND THE GLOBAL JUSTICE MOVEMENT

Throughout the course of the twentieth century, and into the early stages of the twenty-first century, it became widely recognized that local, state, and national (or federal) institutions of social control were no longer sufficient for the challenges arising in an increasingly globalized world. The expanding adoption of transnational, international, and global institutions to address a broad spectrum of harmful activities—from cross-border trafficking to crimes of war—has been one of the defining attributes of the contemporary era. But the international financial institutions operate with a singular absence of effective accountability and oversight.

Controlling international financial institutions

No international institutions or tribunals specifically have jurisdiction over, take complaints on, or adjudicate the broad range of harmful activities engaged in by the international financial institutions. Unlike most organizations, where there are checks and balances or some institutional entity to which they must answer, international financial institutions have no formal external monitoring system. While states are, at least ideally, bound by international laws and treaties, international financial institutions are currently not included as actors that fall under the jurisdiction of these laws and treaties or any controlling agency. Neither the International Court of Justice (a court for states), nor the International Criminal Court (a court for individuals), exercise jurisdiction over these types of organizations. The powerful countries that dominate these institutions—notably, the United States and Western European countries—are highly unlikely to call them to account for their harmful activities, since their policies and practices are aligned with and advance the economic interests of these countries. Unlike most organizations, where there are checks and balances or a populace to which they answer, international financial institutions have no formal external monitoring system.

Formal or legal efforts to control international financial institutions harms or criminalities must contend with the legalistic challenges of establishing direct connections between the implemented policies and the harms generated. This too is problematic when one considers the needs for *actus reas* (save for civil liability) and *mens rea* (guilty mind) speaking to intent. Some existing treaties and resolutions would seem to prohibit some of the harms generated by international financial institutions through the manipulation and forced restructuring of local economies and ownership structures. Nonetheless, they remain forms of "soft" laws as they lack any enforcement mechanism beyond moral and ethical obligations (see Appendix D for a more detailed discussion).

International financial institutions are obliged to some extent to adhere to international norms and laws relating to human rights. Given that they operate as specialized units of the United Nations, they are bound to customary law and the United Nations Charter. The Charter states that the specialized institutions set up intergovernmental agreements within their bylaws to adhere to and are bound to the United Nations Economic and Social Council (Toussaint 2005). Also, the global North countries that are members of and fund these intergovernmental agencies—international financial institutions in the case here—share the responsibility for the actions of those agencies.

In one interpretation, since the early 1970s, the U.S. Congress has taken some initiatives to exercise control over the harmful practices of the international financial institutions, including the World Bank (Dauagirdas 2013). In part, Congress has been responding to lobbying initiatives of NGOs focused upon environmental and human rights issues. Since Congress must appropriate the U.S. contribution to World Bank funding it does have some leverage. But any such oversight has been quite limited at best, in part due to the low salience and visibility of international financial institutions to American voters, as well as the fact that World Bank officials cannot be subpoenaed to testify before Congress. Of course a large proportion of members of Congress favor neo-liberal markets and corporate or finance sector interests over other considerations.

International financial institutions have also been highly complicit in corruption in global South countries. Here again, there are a host of international instruments that have been created to address the general issue, yet these instruments lack direct application to international financial institutions (see Appendix D for more details). Of course it is something of a paradox that the international financial institutions—and especially the World Bank—have declared themselves to be leaders in the battle against corruption, especially that occurring in global South countries.

The International Labour Organization (ILO) Conventions 107 and 169 also note that states as well as organizations such as the international financial institutions have a legal obligation to recognize indigenous peoples' rights and to grant informed consent to policies that directly impact upon their lives. This is more of a moral and ethical obligation with a lack of effective enforcement mechanisms. The international financial institutions are not party members or signatories of the above-noted charters, treaties, and resolutions and in many cases complaints and requests in relation to the International Labour Convention do not lead to any effective response.

Given the reality of the structure of international financial institutions, it is highly unlikely that states with the most influence and vested interests would attempt to apply the international conventions identified above to actors within the international financial institutions, much less attempt to hold these institutions accountable. There are international norms and rules that could potentially be applied to international financial institutions' officials (see Appendix D for a more detailed discussion). Nonetheless, within the context of the realpolitik or geopolitical interests of the international political community and the global economy, it is highly unlikely that formal legal, moral, or ethical initiatives will be issued against international financial institutions. This is unfortunate, due to their complicity in and facilitation of conditions conducive to corruption, human rights violations, environmental damages and other devastating forms of harm. Altogether, there is a lack of applicable and enforceable formal responses to the harms generated by international financial institutions, directly and indirectly.

On the other hand, we should note that approaches to the development and promotion of international treaties and laws are brokered within the select and elite international political community. Individuals representing the interests of the global North and Western countries dominate this process. As such, efforts to promote a legal response to crimes of globalization contribute to the practice of governing through crime. This is so whether or not it is intended. A "grand mythology" of the power of international law is promoted.

The idea of holding international financial institutions formally accountable at this time may be unrealistic and potentially counter-productive. It is highly unlikely that international financial institutions will be willing to self-regulate and comply with extant human rights standards or to ending their support and facilitation of corrupt regimes and practices given the geopolitical environment within which they operate. These institutions typically claim that human rights concerns are outside their scope. However, a recent statement by Rachael Kyte (2011), Vice President for Sustainable Development of the World Bank Group, conceded that these institutions were often blighted by corruption, environmental degradations, and a general disregard for local communities. The human rights obligations of the World Bank were conceded by its own General Counsel, but the legal opinion circulated by this officer was largely greeted by silence (Sarfaty 2012: pp. 63–70). The Bank's board resists adopting human rights initiatives if there is opposition from one of its member countries, which is what happens.

Controlling crimes of globalization: broader challenges

Acknowledging the issues and problems related to international financial institutions policies and practices is a crucial first step forward. The needed changes within the organizational structures are not likely to occur without a broader shift in the neo-liberalism ideology that undergirds the culture and practices of these institutions. Additionally, with the strong discourse of "development" and poverty reduction that supports the broader "regime of truth," there is little room for other competing voices. When the legitimacy of such practices is questioned, more often than not symbolic gestures are introduced in an attempt to appease dissenting voices. Substantive initiatives addressing the broader problems of socio-economic inequalities and environmental harms are typically absent. For example, in response to the growing criticisms of the World Bank's role in promoting and sponsoring loans for open mine development, coal production, and other significantly harmful environmental projects (extractive markets), a new extractives-for-development (E4D) initiative, called the "knowledge sharing platform," was launched. The aim, according to the International Finance Corporation, is to address the failings of and negative consequences of projects by allowing for their more efficient and effective "management" (Bretton Woods Project 2012). The stakeholders involved include governments, civil society organizations, industry associations, academic organizations and development agencies. This group of stakeholders is led by the World Bank's Sustainable Development and Poverty Reduction & Economic Management (PREM) along with the World Bank Institute. Several publications have been produced by this group, which is aimed at "better governance" of extraction sites. An Extractive Industries (EI) Source Book claims to offer technical advice to "decision-makers" in "non-economically powered" states (2013). While this initiative may appear to be addressing issues associated with the extraction and development faced by many countries where the World Bank's funded projects are undertaken, such a response and program does little to address the environmental costs or the impact on local communities of industry "development."

Civil society, the global justice movement, and local protest movements

Ultimately, our concern here is with identifying the optimal strategies that could prevent or at least constrain international financial institution policies and practices that cause significant harm to citizens of developing countries, to the environment, and to the political economy itself. We have set forth an argument for regarding these policies and practices of the international financial institutions as a form of crime. The potential for effective accountability of international financial institutions can probably only be brought about by civil society social activism.

To date, global justice (or anti-globalization) activists and their protest rallies have been the principal entities holding international financial institutions accountable for their harmful policies and practices. Scholars of social movements, globalization, and related phenomena have noted that in the increased era of global connectivity, local concerns are becoming more and more linked to global patterns of power (Escobar 2000; Mason 2012; Pleyers 2011). Social movements operate at both the local and global levels. Escobar (2000) has suggested persuasively in his work on the global social movement that in the context of transnational social movements, various collective identities intersect. These identities become transformed into, potentially, a global collective identity, giving additional power to a resistance mechanism against the international financial institutions' policies (Langman and Morris 2012). The ultimate effectiveness of civil society challenges to these policies will depend importantly upon whether or not a global collective identity develops and expands.

There is by now a large literature on an emerging global civil society and the many entities that claim to offer hope of fundamental reforms or structural transformations toward producing a more just and equitable world (e.g., Prashad 2012; Stroup 2012; von Bulow 2010). Will the World Social Forum—which has met at Porto Alegre in Brazil and at other sites—become a foundation for successfully challenging crimes of globalization? Can international non-governmental organizations (INGOs)—such as Amnesty International, Human Rights Watch, Greenpeace, Oxfam, and Transparency International—be ultimately effective in this realm? Will a global civil society of transnational networks of activists make a difference? These are large questions which we cannot do justice to here, but which need to be taken into account in any ongoing dialogue about crimes of globalization.

Local resistance has also increased in areas directly affected by international financial institution policies and investments. For example, in November of 2011, 20,000 citizens in the Peruvian state of Cajamarca demonstrated against a Conga mine proposed by Minera Yanacoch, a mining company owned by Newmont, a large United States multinational mining corporation (Bretton Woods Project 2012). The demonstrators included 8,000 local farmers blockading a town amidst concerns that the state was pressuring locals to sign agreements without consultation with the locals that would be harmed by these agreements. In response, the government suspended the construction of the mine and announced it would seek international consultants to evaluate the impact of the mine project.

Other protests by locals include the recent April, 2013, demonstrations in Bhubaneswar, New Delhi, and Bangalore, India, against World Bank policies and projects (*New Indian Express* 2013). There was widespread concern that harmful and corrupt public–private sector activities promoted by the World Bank would occur. More specifically, these World Bank initiatives included illegally closing down various public sector programs relating to education and health, funding environmentally unsustainable projects, and complicity in basic human rights abuses. The protestors stated that thousands of people have been forcibly displaced and the Bank's programs have destroyed parts of the environment, including land aimed at forestry sector development. As one protester stated, "[t]he World Bank Group claims that it has lent around $26 billion to India between 2009 and 2013. However, these funds are spent through different anti-community policies, programmes and projects and has helped the corporate sectors only. Poverty has increased during this period" (*New Indian Express*, June 3, 2013: p. 1).

In Kosovo, citizen advocacy groups have joined together to protest the World Bank's funding of coal plants (Guay 2013). They have released public health ads and used social media in connection with this protest campaign. Coverage was intense enough that the public outcry by the general population forced the World Bank to respond with an op-ed in the largest newspaper in India. The most recent Bank project includes a $58 million Partial Risk Guarantee (PRG) for a proposed Kosovo Power Project (Mainhardt and Sinani 2013: p. 1). This project calls for building a new 600-megawatt lignite coal-based power plant, known as Kosova Re Power Project, and expanding open-pit coal mining operations. The project has a huge potential to cause devastating environmental harm to waterways upon which people in this region of Kosovo are wholly dependent.

Public protests have occurred in other countries. In Egypt protests against the former Morsi regime addressed its acceptance of a major $4.8 billion loan from the International Monetary Fund. The loan was conditioned on mandated tax increases and subsidy cuts on food and other daily subsistence needs of Egyptian citizens. Such conditions are similar to those accepted by the former President Mubarak's regime that was forced out of office during the Arab Spring uprising in 2011. Egypt under Mubarak had adopted the neo-liberal policies of the international financial institutions (Marfleet 2013). Many of the consequences of International Monetary Fund–mandated structural reforms accepted by Mubarak were a central part of the populations' dissatisfaction that contributed to the Arab Spring uprising against his regime. In July, 2013, millions of Egyptians took to the streets to protest against the Morsi regime and brought about its provisional end (Hubbard *et al.* 2013). Although a range of grievances against the Morsi regime and the Muslim Brotherhood were involved, it is reasonable to surmise that anger in relation to dealings with international financial institutions played some role. The success of popularist uprisings in Egypt in 2011 and 2013 in bringing down regimes viewed as not acting in the interest of the Egyptian people may well inspire future activist protests against the policies and practices of the international financial institutions.

Through the expanded use of social media, activists and local communities are creating websites dedicated to exposing international financial institutions policies and practices that have hugely harmful consequences. Such websites receive thousands of hits and accordingly contribute to the potential of an expanding global movement against international financial institutions. For example, the World

Development Movement's (2013: 1) site states that "[t]he World Bank has a long history of funding projects that are destructive to the environment and undermine human rights, investing in projects regardless of their devastating impacts both on local populations and on our planet." They provide an interactive map that allows users to follow projects funded by international financial institutions that have caused devastating harm. These projects range from the Guyana-Omai Gold Mine in Brazil, to the Kedung Ombo Multipurpose Dam and Irrigation Project in Indonesia, to the Kumtor Mining Project in Kyrgyzstan. An activist group calling itself "third world traveler" uses a website to bring attention to a harmful project in San Marcos, Guatemala. The Glamis Gold mining company, a Canadian company with headquarters in Reno, Nevada, was given a $45 million loan from the World Bank to construct and operate an open-pit gold and silver mine there. During the initial phase of construction, over 2,000 indigenous farmers and villagers blocked a convoy traveling on the Pan-American Highway carrying mining equipment from reaching the Marlin site (Mychalejko 2005: p. 2). The blockade lasted 40 days. At that point Guatemala's Interior Ministry deployed the military and security forces to the protest site to protect the interests of investors. While this protest was unsuccessful at stopping the implementation of the mine, monitoring of the Guatemala mine project is ongoing. Canada's Mine Watch is one website viewed by thousands where mine-related damage is reported.

In a more formal sense, local protests have resulted in twenty current cases being filed at the Compliance Advisor/Omsbudsman (CAO) office of the World Bank. Local groups have organized and brought forth complaints against various projects that have led to or will lead to serious environmental, social and cultural harms. In 2012, the CAO handled more complaints and requests for audits than at any time in their twelve-year history. The CAO addressed a total of 33 cases, of which 19 were carried over from 2011 and 14 were new cases in 2012 (CAO 2012: p. 6). According to A World Bank compliance report (CAO 2012: p. 6):

> Fifty-five percent of 2012 cases involved local civil society organizations and 27 percent were filed by individuals or community members without the assistance of other organizations . . . Cases

were distributed globally, with the majority relating to projects in Latin America (34 percent) followed by Africa (24 percent) and East Asia (21 percent).

Complaints related to projects in Cambodia, Cameroon, Chad, Colombia, Georgia, India, Indonesia, the Republic of Kosovo, Mexico, Mozambique, Nicaragua, Panama, Papua New Guinea, Peru, the Philippines, Turkey, Uganda, and the Africa region. Of these, three cases were dropped, fourteen remain active, seven were transferred to the compliance sector to be evaluated and two were closed.

Activist complaints about development projects have been broad-ranging, with the dominant complaints directed at economic and environmental degradation. For example, in 2011, two local communities in the Philippines brought a complaint over the $9.5 million equity investment of the Canadian mining Company Mindoro Resource Ltd. They claimed that the project would destroy forest vital to their social, environmental, and cultural well-being. Another case involves two communities in Peru that claim that the Maple Energy Company that received $40 million from the World Bank Group in 2007 to drill for new oil caused mass spillage, resulting in numerous health and environmental problems (Bretton Woods Project 2012). The Comité por la Defensa del Agua y el Páramo de Santurbán, an NGO, filed its case in June 2012, alleging that the World Bank's private lending arm's $20 million investment in the project, the Greystar mine in Columbia, would result in massive environmental, economic, and social harms.

Some global South countries are also responding to the harmful policies of the international financial institutions by refusing to accept mandated policies and turning to other financial sources or by paying back their loans in full early and requesting the institutions to remove their oversight agencies. For example, dating back to 2007, the late President Hugo Chávez of Venezuela announced that his country was removing itself as a member of the World Bank Group and the International Monetary Fund. This announcement was made after Venezuela repaid its debts to the World Bank Group five years in advance of schedule, reducing the interest by $8 million. The formal closing of the regional International Monetary Fund offices then occurred in the latter half of

2007. Following suit, Nicaraguan President Daniel Ortega stated that his country would also "get out of that prison" of the International Monetary Fund debt and began negotiating an exit strategy to leave the fund. And in 2007, Ecuadorean President Rafael Correa asked the World Bank's representative to leave his country after it paid off its debt in advance. Argentina also has paid back billions of dollars to the International Monetary Fund in an effort to reduce the control and impact of the international financial institutions' policies. More recently, Latvia, in late December 2012, paid back the entire $9.9 billion 2008 rescue loan to the International Monetary Fund, claiming they wanted to make their own economic policies and decisions and not be held to outside pressures. In January, 2013, Ukrainian Prime Minister Mykola Azarov stated that the country would not concede to demands made by the International Monetary Fund to hike gas tariffs and would instead seek funds elsewhere to finance outstanding payments to the International Monetary Fund (Gorchinskava 2013). Likewise, in August 2013, Hungary repaid the remainder of its 2.15 billion Euros outstanding debt to the International Monetary Fund to end what Prime Minister Viktor Orban called "undue foreign influence over its economic policies" (Dunai and Szakacs 2013: p. 1). All of these initiatives could be regarded as reflections of growing recognition that global South countries have been victims of the crimes of the international financial institutions. The leaders of such countries are likely to be under increasing pressure to accede to perceptions of their citizenry in regard to such crimes.

Although clear-cut successes have been relatively few to date, the overall protest campaigns are a step in the right direction towards prioritizing people over corporate vested interests and the promotion of the neo-liberal agenda. Coalitions of civil society organizations, indigenous movements and international environmental and human rights organizations continue to challenge the World Bank and International Monetary Fund's projects, policies, and demands. However, while some controversial projects supported and funded by international financial institutions are now subjected to greater scrutiny, the mass power and influence that these institutions have over states' policies and economies and the intersection with corporate interests continues to pose a great hindrance to the potential of social movements. A sustainable future for all people depends upon a broad global movement that is committed to the realization of that objective.

Cosmopolitanism and crimes of globalization

In our view, a successful global social movement in response to the crimes of the international financial institutions depends upon broader adoption of a cosmopolitan outlook. The term *cosmopolitan* has been invoked in different ways. It is an ideology expressing that all of humanity belongs to a single moral community—an ideology for "global citizenship." The notion of a cosmopolitan outlook is one that views humans as part of a world community with allegiances to all human beings, transcending particularistic attachments, and takes into account the impact of globalization on local and national issues. Such an ideology is not new. For centuries, philosophers and jurists have speculated on the necessary conditions for achieving enduring peace and justice between nations (Friedrichs 2007). Immanuel Kant (1795), in his essay *Perpetual Peace*, suggested *ius cosmopoliticum* (cosmopolitan law/right) be a guiding principle to protect people from war—grounded in the belief of universal hospitality. In the contemporary era interest in the idea of cosmopolitanism re-emerged after World War II (Rothe 2009). The post-World War II form of cosmopolitanism took place in both formal and informal political realms.

Cosmopolitanism is often associated with more than just an ideology for a global citizenship. It has also come to be associated with global governance. The question of global governance is certain to become progressively more urgent and more widely discussed during the course of the twenty-first century, and it is quite imperative that students of international crime and law engage with the evolving transnational discussion on this question. The key terms here—including "global" and "governance"—are invoked in different ways, with popular writers tending to equate global governance with "government" whereas academics and international practitioners tend to equate it with complex public and private structures and processes (Friedrichs 2007). The idea of global governance, a centralized entity that in some sense governs the world, strikes many commentators as a utopian fantasy and as a frightening nightmare if actually realized. A "world government" is profoundly problematic for those on both the conservative and the progressive ends of the ideological spectrum. For conservatives, the concession of national sovereignty is especially objectionable; for progressives, the notion of such a concentration of power is especially objectionable. But global governance in contemporary discourse transcends simplistic notions of world government. Global governance is perceived as likely to include the development of new forms of cosmopolitan citizenship and institutional hierarchy (Khagram 2006: p. 110). A global civil society is one dimension of evolving global governance and, in one view, can serve as an antidote to the activities of predatory financial institutions, from those at the domestic level to those at the international level. We suggest that the notion of a collective identity and consciousness founded on core principles of universal human rights and justice (including economic justice) is the best hope that disempowered and marginalized populations have to counteract the currently prevailing forces of neo-liberal economic policies and state subjugation.

A Gaian global order

Surely many observers and commentators regard the present architecture of the global political economy, including the role played by the international financial institutions, as profoundly entrenched, enduring and necessary. But there are many others, including ourselves, who regard it as neither sustainable nor just. Proposals have been put forth aimed at creating a global system that is more just. For example, Ross Jackson (2012) has proposed a "Gaian" system for the global economic system. It is based on a perspective of symbiosis and interconnectedness—where the earth is a self-regulating, complex system that maintains an environment optimal for life and where the chemical equilibrium is dynamically steady due to the presence of life. Jackson proposes that this scientific paradigm will change the values and priorities of systems where humans are recognized as interconnected social beings rather than atomistic individuals. More relevant to crimes of globalization, Jackson proposes an international system based on the Gaian model:

Gaian World Order. At the top of the sphere of influence and political/ economic power are the world citizens that adopt the decisions within an elected council. Beneath the council is an appointed congress, drawn on from member states. There is then a commission of oversight and a court of justice to hear issues that may arise from the last section of the order: a clearing union, trade organization, development bank and a resource board. The council would consist of a small elected group of "wise elders" that would be empowered to overrule any congress or law deemed not in the interest of the planet. The congress would be an assembly of delegates appointed by Gaian league governments. The commission would be headed by a Secretary General, much as with the United Nations, creating resolutions that define laws for states. The Gaian trade organization would replace the current World Trade Organization with the priority of fair trade versus the current system of "free"—actually rigged—trade. The clearing union would regulate and settle international trade disputes and the development bank would replace the International Monetary Fund and the World Bank, funding non-exploitive "development" using local currencies and focusing on local communities. The proposed resource board would administer resources, based on the belief in ecological sustainability and absolute scarcity of resources, in the interests of the entire planet—not an Empire or a select set of states as our current system is dominated by (Jackson 2012). Is such a vision simply a utopian fantasy? Perhaps it is. But we adhere to the strongly held conviction that alternatives to the present global political economy must be envisioned and pursued.

The role of students of crime and criminal justice

It is our view that students of crime and criminal justice have a role to play in the evolving worldwide campaign against crimes of globalization. Ideally, further attention to such crimes is promoted through engagement with "news-making criminology" or "public criminology" (Barak 2012; Loader and Sparks 2011). One of our objectives for this book is to contribute to educating students of crime and criminal justice to become more aware of and more knowledgeable about crimes of globalization and the formidable challenges that arise in relation to their control. Ideally, then, as opportunities arise to engage in news-making criminology in relation to crimes of globalization criminologists are better prepared to contribute a specifically criminological framework for making sense of such crimes of globalization. For example, a failed World Bank or International Monetary Fund initiative in a developing country receives significant media and public attention. Students of crime and criminal justice can demonstrate how such a failed initiative is indeed crime, and how criminal justice entities have a role to play in response to such crime.

Increasingly, a public criminology of crimes of globalization incorporates "subaltern" perspectives: i.e., the vantage point of victimized constituencies in developing countries. A public criminology, if it is to be effective, has to identify external political and social circumstances that produce a context receptive to embracing progressive and transformative social policy. Ideally, as well, a public criminology in relation to crimes of globalization contributes on the one hand to dissemination (popularization) of core knowledge about this phenomenon, as well as the promotion of public discourse (democratic deliberation) about the policy options in relation to effectively responding to crimes of globalization (Kalleberg 2005). Ideally it contributes, at least in some modest way, to an ultimate abandonment of policies and practices harmful to vast numbers of people around the globe, and the adoption of an alternative model of globalization that fosters greater equality, sustainable conditions and better lives for all.

For a student or researcher of crimes of globalization, the key question still remains: what can be done? As citizens and as criminologists, what can we do to constrain and control the international financial institutions' prioritization of economic interests of corporations and major stakeholders over those of the well-being of all citizens, protection of basic human rights, and the reduction of gross economic inequality? Is this an impossible task? Will there always be some form of crimes of globalization? In the final analysis, the answer to this question is surely yes. But we offer here a few concluding thoughts on how students of crime and criminology—and, indeed, all concerned citizens and stakeholders—can respond to the very large problem of crimes of globalization.

Victimization by crimes of globalization can be reduced by the following general strategies that apply to each of us at the individual and personal level:

1. Continue to expand the awareness of crimes of globalization. It is only through global awareness that public outrage can occur. A critical mass of globalized public outrage can compel key stakeholders to re-evaluate their priorities and practices.
2. Work towards attaining some sense of commonality based on shared human values. If each of us starts with ourselves in living out this worldview and philosophy, it can and will grow, even if it takes several generations to spread to a level wherein the majority of people share the same common outlook, goals, or vision.
3. Recognize our role in the promotion and facilitation of crimes of globalization with the demands for consumer products associated with projects that are displacing and socially, economically, and culturally harming others across the globe.
4. Demand and work for accountability of international financial institutions in their active and passive roles in facilitating crimes of globalization and for social restoration for the areas and peoples that have been victimized by the crimes.

There is no magic answer or quick policy fix for crimes of globalization. It is an ongoing problem that requires diligence, commitment, and a change in ideology, praxis, priorities, and social relations. But we believe that there is much at stake in students of crime and criminal justice becoming more fully engaged with the issues we have addressed here.

APPENDICES

A: Debt ratios of non-Western countries 2008–2010

Country	Total external debt (millions of U.S. dollars)	Ratio of external debt to exports of goods and services (%)	Ratio of total external debt to GNI (%)
Afghanistan	2,297	67	21
Albania	4,736	115	39
Algeria	5,276	6	3
Angola	18,562	26	26
Argentina	127,849	158	40
Armenia	6,103	238	40
Azerbaijan	6,974	25	16
Bangladesh	24,963	132	26
Belarus	25,726	83	47
Belize	1,045	129	84
Benin	1,221	101	18
Bhutan	898	109	69
Bolivia	5,267	75	31
Bosnia and Herzegovina	8,457	120	47
Botswana	1,709	28	13
Brazil	346,978	155	20

Bulgaria	48,077	170	102
Burkina Faso	2,053	225	25
Burundi	537	418	39
Cambodia	4,676	75	46
Cameroon	2,964	47	13
Cape Verde	857	136	56
Central African Republic	385	119	19
Chad	1,733	54	27
Chile	86,349	108	52
Columbia	63,064	145	126
Comoros	485	714	91
Democratic Republic of Congo	5,774	151	52
Republic of the Congo	3,781	46	47
Costa Rica	8,849	65	29
Côte d'Ivoire	11,430	95	52
Djibouti	751	176	65
Dominica	267	163	74
Dominican Republic	13,045	107	28
Ecuador	14,815	75	26
Egypt	34,844	107	28
El Salvador	11,069	201	53
Eritrea	1,010	1,237	57
Fiji	452	28	15
Gabon	2,331	18	21
The Gambia	470	157	64
Georgia	9,238	225	80
Ghana	8,368	103	30
Grenada	576	309	96
Guatemala	14,340	139	37
Guinea	2,923	211	78
Guinea-Bissau	1,095	766	130
Guyana	1,354	131	57
Haiti	492	55	8
Honduras	4,168	27	30
India	290,282	91	20
Indonesia	179,064	114	32

(continued)

(continued)

Country	Total external debt (millions of U.S. dollars)	Ratio of external debt to exports of goods and services (%)	Ratio of total external debt to GNI (%)
Jamaica	13,865	232	107
Jordan	7,822	60	30
Kazakhstan	118,723	181	104
Kenya	8,400	102	28
Kosovo	342	35	6
Kyrgyz Republic	3,984	150	86
Lao PDR	5,559	296	92
Latvia	39,555	280	139
Lebanon	24,293	102	70
Lesotho	726	43	31
Liberia	228	37	31
Lithuania	29,602	116	75
Macedonia	5,804	130	63
Madagascar	2,295	75	26
Malawi	922	82	20
Malaysia	81,497	36	39
Maldives	1,229	129	95
Mali	2,326	94	27
Mauritania	2,461	131	71
Mauritius	1,076	20	11
Mexico	200,081	68	20
Moldova	4,615	154	74
Mongolia	2,444	83	48
Montenegro	1,554	71	37
Morocco	25,403	82	29
Mozambique	4,124	137	44
Nepal	3,702	203	27
Nicaragua	4,786	150	78
Niger	1,127	107	21
Nigeria	7,883	10	4
Pakistan	56,773	218	33
Panama	11,412	62	50
Papua New Guinea	5,882	101	70
Paraguay	4,938	55	30
Peru	36,271	100	28

Philippines	72,337	115	40
Romania	121,505	205	70
Russian Federation	384,740	80	27
Rwanda	795	137	15
Samoa	308	160	58
São Tomé and Príncipe	170	777	90
Senegal	3,677	95	28
Serbia	32,222	229	76
Seychelles	1,510	170	189
Sierra Leone	778	207	41
Solomon Islands	215	68	41
South Africa	45,165	46	15
Sri Lanka	20,452	201	47
St. Kitts and Nevis	203	97	39
St. Lucia	464	81	53
St. Vincent and Grenadines	261	127	47
Sudan	21,846	199	41
Swaziland	616	27	20
Syrian Arab Republic	4,729	25	9
Tajikistan	2,955	196	57
Tanzania	8,664	148	40
Thailand	71,263	34	26
Togo	1,728	154	61
Tonga	144	260	41
Tunisia	21,584	86	53
Turkey	293,872	180	43
Turkmenistan	422	3	2
Uganda	2,994	90	19
Ukraine	117,128	157	82
Uruguay	11,347	113	34
Uzbekistan	7,404	56	22
Vanuatu	148	54	23
Venezuela	55,572	70	16
Vietnam	35,139	49	38
Yemen	6,324	71	24
Zambia	3,689	63	28
Zimbabwe	5,016	230	92

Source: The World Bank (2012)

B: Countries included in the World Bank Extraction Industry Transparency Initiative reports

Country	Years covered	Sectors covered
Afghanistan	2010	Mining
Afghanistan	2009	Mining
Afghanistan	2008	Mining
Albania	2010	Oil, Gas, Mining
Albania	2009	Oil, Mining
Azerbaijan	2011	Oil, Gas, Mining
Azerbaijan	2010	Oil, Gas, Mining
Azerbaijan	2009	Oil, Gas, Mining
Azerbaijan	2008	Oil, Gas
Azerbaijan	2007	Oil, Gas
Azerbaijan	2006	Oil, Gas
Azerbaijan	2005	Oil, Gas
Azerbaijan	2004	Oil, Gas
Azerbaijan	2003	Oil, Gas
Burkina Faso	2010	Mining
Burkina Faso	2009	Mining
Burkina Faso	2008	Mining
Cameroon	2010	Oil, Mining
Cameroon	2009	Oil, Mining
Cameroon	2008	Oil, Gas, Mining
Cameroon	2007	Oil, Gas, Mining
Cameroon	2006	Oil, Gas, Mining
Cameroon	2005	Oil, Gas
Cameroon	2004	Oil, Gas
Cameroon	2003	Oil, Gas
Cameroon	2002	Oil, Gas
Cameroon	2001	Oil, Gas
Central African Republic	2010	Mining
Central African Republic	2009	Mining
Central African Republic	2008	Mining
Central African Republic	2007	Mining
Central African Republic	2006	Mining
Chad	2011	Oil, Gas, Mining
Chad	2010	Oil, Gas, Mining
Chad	2009	Oil, Gas, Mining

Chad	2008	Oil, Gas, Mining
Chad	2007	Oil, Gas, Mining
Côte d'Ivoire	2011	Oil, Gas, Mining
Côte d'Ivoire	2010	Oil, Gas, Mining
Côte d'Ivoire	2009	Oil, Gas, Mining
Côte d'Ivoire	2008	Oil, Gas, Mining
Côte d'Ivoire	2007	Oil, Gas
Côte d'Ivoire	2006	Oil, Gas
Democratic Republic of Congo	2010	Mining, Oil, Gas
Democratic Republic of Congo	2009	Oil, Gas, Mining
Democratic Republic of Congo	2008	Oil, Gas, Mining
Democratic Republic of Congo	2007	Oil, Gas, Mining
Gabon	2010	Oil, Gas, Mining
Gabon	2009	Oil, Gas, Mining
Gabon	2008	Oil, Mining
Gabon	2007	Oil, Gas
Gabon	2006	Oil, Gas
Gabon	2005	Oil, Gas, Mining
Gabon	2004	Oil, Gas
Ghana	2011	Mining, Oil, Gas
Ghana	2010	Mining, Oil, Gas
Ghana	2009	Mining
Ghana	2008	Mining
Ghana	2007	Mining
Ghana	2006	Mining
Ghana	2005	Mining
Ghana	2004	Mining
Guinea	2010	Mining
Guinea	2009	Mining
Guinea	2008	Mining
Guinea	2007	Mining
Guinea	2006	Mining
Guinea	2005	Mining
Indonesia	2009	Oil, Gas, Mining, Other
Iraq	2010	Oil, Gas
Iraq	2009	Oil
Kazakhstan	2011	Oil, Gas, Mining
Kazakhstan	2010	Oil, Gas, Mining

(continued)

(continued)

Country	Years covered	Sectors covered
Kazakhstan	2009	Oil, Gas, Mining
Kazakhstan	2008	Oil, Gas, Mining
Kazakhstan	2007	Oil, Gas, Mining
Kazakhstan	2006	Oil, Gas, Mining
Kazakhstan	2005	Oil
Kyrgyz Republic	2011	Mining, Oil, Gas
Kyrgyz Republic	2010	Mining, Oil, Gas
Kyrgyz Republic	2009	Mining
Kyrgyz Republic	2008	Mining
Kyrgyz Republic	2007	Mining
Kyrgyz Republic	2006	Mining
Kyrgyz Republic	2005	Mining
Kyrgyz Republic	2004	Mining
Liberia	2011	Oil, Gas, Mining, Other
Liberia	2010	Oil, Mining, Other
Liberia	2009	Oil, Mining, Other
Liberia	2008	Oil, Mining, Other
Madagascar	2010	Oil, Gas, Mining
Madagascar	2009	Mining
Madagascar	2008	Mining
Madagascar	2007	Mining
Mali	2010	Mining
Mali	2009	Mining, Oil
Mali	2008	Mining
Mali	2007	Mining
Mali	2006	Mining
Mauritania	2009	Oil, Mining
Mauritania	2008	Oil, Mining
Mauritania	2007	Oil, Mining
Mauritania	2006	Oil, Mining
Mauritania	2005	Oil, Mining
Mongolia	2011	Mining
Mongolia	2010	Oil, Mining
Mongolia	2009	Oil, Mining
Mongolia	2008	Oil, Mining
Mongolia	2007	Mining
Mongolia	2006	Mining
Mozambique	2010	Oil, Gas, Mining

Mozambique	2009	Oil, Gas, Mining
Mozambique	2008	Gas, Mining
Niger	2010	Oil, Gas, Mining
Niger	2009	Mining
Niger	2008	Mining
Niger	2007	Mining
Niger	2006	Mining
Niger	2005	Mining
Nigeria	2011	Oil, Gas
Nigeria	2010	Oil, Gas
Nigeria	2009	Oil, Gas
Nigeria	2008	Oil, Gas
Nigeria	2007	Oil, Gas
Nigeria	2006	Oil, Gas
Nigeria	2005	Oil, Gas
Nigeria	2004	Oil, Gas
Nigeria	2003	Oil, Gas
Nigeria	2002	Oil, Gas
Nigeria	2001	Oil, Gas
Nigeria	2000	Oil, Gas
Nigeria	1999	Oil, Gas
Norway	2011	Oil, Gas
Norway	2010	Oil, Gas
Norway	2009	Oil, Gas
Norway	2008	Oil, Gas
Peru	2010	Oil, Gas, Mining
Peru	2009	Oil, Gas, Mining
Peru	2008	Oil, Gas, Mining
Peru	2007	Oil, Gas, Mining
Peru	2006	Oil, Gas, Mining
Peru	2005	Oil, Gas, Mining
Peru	2004	Oil, Gas, Mining
Republic of the Congo	2011	Oil, Gas
Republic of the Congo	2010	Oil, Gas
Republic of the Congo	2009	Oil, Gas
Republic of the Congo	2008	Oil, Gas
Republic of the Congo	2007	Oil, Gas
Republic of the Congo	2006	Oil, Gas

(continued)

(continued)

Country	Years covered	Sectors covered
Republic of the Congo	2005	Oil, Gas
Republic of the Congo	2004	Oil, Gas
Sierra Leone	2010	Oil, Gas, Mining
Sierra Leone	2009	Oil, Gas, Mining
Sierra Leone	2008	Mining, Oil, Gas
Sierra Leone	2007	Mining
Sierra Leone	2006	Mining
Tanzania	2010	Oil, Gas, Mining
Tanzania	2009	Oil, Gas, Mining
Timor-Leste	2011	Oil, Gas
Timor-Leste	2010	Oil, Gas
Timor-Leste	2009	Oil, Gas
Timor-Leste	2008	Oil, Gas
Togo	2011	Mining, Oil, Other
Togo	2010	Mining, Oil, Other
Yemen	2007	Oil, Gas
Yemen	2006	Oil, Gas
Yemen	2005	Oil, Gas
Zambia	2010	Mining
Zambia	2009	Mining
Zambia	2008	Mining

Source: Extractive Industries Transparency Initiative (2013)

C: Current water privatization projects in approval stages

Date disclosed	Company name	Country	IFC loan (millions of U.S. dollars)	IFC equity (millions of U.S. dollars)	Total IFC investment (millions of U.S. dollars)
4/30/2013	MWC	Philippines	150		150
4/30/2013	MWC	Philippines			
3/25/2013	Izsu	Turkey			
3/25/2013	Izsu	Turkey	35.89		35.89
2/5/2013	Moya Indonesia	Indonesia			
2/5/2013	Moya Indonesia	Indonesia	23.66	8.74	32.4
8/23/2012	Organica Water	World Region			
8/23/2012	Organica Water	World Region		5	5
5/16/2012	Aqualia	World Region			
5/16/2012	Aqualia	World Region			
4/17/2012	Metito Holdings	MENA Region	50		50
4/17/2012	Metito Holdings	MENA Region			

Source: International Finance Corporation (2013b)

D: International treaties, resolutions, and laws

Some existing treaties and resolutions would seem to prohibit some of the harms generated by international financial institutions through the manipulation and forced restructuring of local economies and ownership structures. These treaties, resolutions and proposed principles include the *1974 Declaration on the Establishment of a New International Economic Order* (UNGA 1974, 3201/s-vii), the *Convention on Economic, Social and Cultural Human Rights* (UNGA 2003a), the Maastricht Guidelines (Van Boven *et al.* 1997), and the *Norms on the Responsibilities of Transnational Corporations and Other Business Enterprises with Regard to Human Rights Agreement* (not adopted) (United Nations Sub-Commission on the Promotion and Protection of Human Rights 2003), and *The Guiding Principles on Business and Human Rights: Implementing the United Nations "Protect, Respect and Remedy" Framework* (UNGA 2011). Nonetheless, these remain forms of "soft" laws as they lack any enforcement mechanism beyond moral and ethical obligations against corruption, especially that occurring in developing countries. They include the *United Nations Convention against Corruption* (UN Office on Drugs and Crime 2004a), the *United Nations Convention against Transnational Organized Crime* (UN Office on Drugs and Crime 2004b), the Council of Europe's *Criminal and Civil Law Conventions on Corruption*, the *Convention of the European Union on the Protection of Its Financial Interests*, the *Convention of the European Union on the Fight against Corruption Involving Officials of the European Communities or Officials of Member States*, the *African Union Convention on Preventing and Combating Corruption*, the *Inter-American Convention against Corruption*, and the *OECD-Convention on Combating Bribery of Foreign Public Officials in International Business Transactions*.

The *Norms on the Responsibilities of Transnational Corporations and Other Business Enterprises with Regard to Human Rights* resolution recognizes that transnational corporations and other business enterprises are also responsible for promoting and securing the human rights set forth in the *Universal Declaration of Human Rights* and they are obligated to respect the responsibilities and norms contained in UN treaties, including the *United Nations Convention against Transnational Organized Crime*. Likewise, *The Guiding Principles on Business and Human Rights:*

Implementing the United Nations "Protect, Respect and Remedy" Framework
(2011: 17/4) states that it is *"Emphasizing* that transnational corporations
and other business enterprises have a responsibility to respect human
rights."

The *United Nations Convention against Corruption* Article 2 (c) states

> [t]hat an "Official of a public international organization" shall
> mean an international civil servant or any person who is author-
> ized by such an organization to act on behalf of that organization.

The *United Nations Convention against Organized Crime* Article 5, 1 states

> [e]ach State Party shall adopt such legislative and other measures as
> may be necessary to establish as criminal offences, when committed
> intentionally including (b) Organizing, directing, aiding, abetting,
> facilitating or counseling the commission of serious crime involv-
> ing an organized criminal group where the knowledge, intent, aim,
> purpose or agreement referred to in paragraph 1 may be inferred
> from objective factual circumstances (Article 5, 2).

The foregoing is limited in its applicability and enforcement as jurisdiction lies within each state's domestic territory. In Article 15, 2 it
proclaims that

> Subject to article 4 of this Convention, a State Party may also estab-
> lish its jurisdiction over any such offence when: (a) The offence is
> committed against a national of that State Party; (b) The offence is
> committed by a national of that State Party.

REFERENCES

Aas, K. F. (2007). *Globalization and Crime*. New York: Sage.

Aas, K. F. (2012). "The Earth Is One but the World Is Not: Criminological Theory and Its Geopolitical Divisions." *Theoretical Criminology*, 16: 5–20.

Aas K. F. (Ed.) (2014). *Crime and Globalization*. Los Angeles, CA: Sage.

Abdou, D. S. and Zaazou, Z. (2013). "The Egyptian Revolution and Post Socio-Economic Impact." *Topics in Middle Eastern and African Economies*, 15(1): 92–115.

Abouharb, M. R. and Cingarelli, D. L. (2006). "The Human Rights Effects of World Bank Structural Adjustment, 1981–2000." *International Studies Quarterly*, 50: 233–262.

Abramsky, S. (2007). *American Furies: Crime, Punishment, and Vengeance in the Age of Mass Imprisonment*. Boston, MA: Beacon Press.

African Development Bank Group (2010). "Hydrological Impacts of Ethiopia's Omo Basin on Kenya's Lake Turkana Water Levels and Fisheries: Final Report." Available online from: <http://www.afdb.org/fileadmin/uploads/afdb/Documents/Compliance-Review/REPORT_NOV_2010_S_AVERY_TURKANA_Small_file.pdf> (Accessed October 9, 2013).

African Union (2003). Convention on Preventing and Combating Corruption. Available online from: <http://www.africa-union.org/root/au/Documents/Treaties/Text/Convention%2520on%2520Combating%2520Corruption.pdf+&cd=1&hl=en&ct=clnk&gl> (Accessed March 12, 2014).

Agnew, R. (2011). *Toward a Unified Criminology: Integrating Assumptions about Crime, People, and Society*. New York: New York University Press.

Agozino, B. (2010). "Editorial: What is Criminology? A Control-Freak Discipline!" *African Journal of Criminology & Justice Studies*, 4: 1–20.

Albanese, J. (2011). *Transnational Crime and the 21st Century*. New York: Oxford University Press.

Alexander, J. C. (2006). *The Civil Sphere*. New York: Oxford University Press.

Alhassan, A. (2011). "IFC Helping Western Multinationals Exploit Ghana's Water Crisis." Available online from: <http://www.brettonwoodsproject. org/art-568911> (Accessed September 4, 2013).

Anheier, H., Kaldor, M., and Glasius, M. (2012). "The Global Civil Society Yearbook: Lessons and Insights 2001–2011." In M. Kaldor, H. L. Moore and S. Selchow (Eds.) *Global Civil Society 2012* (pp. 2–27), London: Palgrave Macmillan.

Auerswald, P. (2012). *The Coming Prosperity: How Entrepreneurs are Transforming the Global Economy*. New York: Oxford University Press.

Babb, S. (2009). *Behind the Development Banks: Washington Politics, World Poverty, and the Wealth of Nations*. Chicago, IL: University of Chicago Press.

Baber, Z. (2008). "A Name for a Stray Dog – Global Civil Society." *International Society*, 23: 237–245.

Badgley, C. (2010). "Cameroon: Pipeline to Prosperity? What Happened to the Project Promoters Called a "Cargo of Hope" for Africans." Available online from: <http://www.pbs.org/frontlineworld/stories/bribe/2010/06/ ten-years-ago-this-month.html> (Accessed September 4, 2013).

Barak, G. (1997). *Integrating Criminologies*. Needham Heights, MA: Allyn and Bacon.

Barak, G. (2012) "Media and Crime." In W. DeKeseredy and M. Dragiewicz (Eds.) *Routledge Handbook of Critical Criminology*. London: Routledge.

Beck, U. (2008). *World at Risk*. Ciaran Cronin (trans.), Malden, MA: Polity Press.

Beirne, P. (1983). "Generalization and Its Discontents: The Comparative Study of Crime." In Barak-Glantz and E. Johnson (Eds.) *Comparative Criminology* (pp. 19–37), Beverly Hills, CA: Sage.

Bernard, T. J. (1990). "Twenty Years of Testing Theories: What Have We Learned and Why?" *Journal of Research in Crime and Delinquency*, 27(4): 325–347.

Black, M. (2007). *The No-Nonsense Guide to International Development*. Oxford: New Internationalist.

Bosshard, P. (2013). "Africa: The World Bank Is Bringing Back Big, Bad Dams." Available online from: <http://allafrica.com/stories/201308121000.html> (Accessed September 4, 2013).

Bosworth, M. and Hoyle, C. (2011). *What Is Criminology?* New York: Oxford University Press.

Bradlow, D. (1996). "The World Bank, the IMF, and Human Rights. See: International Monetary Fund IMF and Human Rights." *Transnational Law and Contemporary Problems*, 6: 47–90.

Brady, D. (2010). "Common Ground for Sociology and the World Bank?" *Contemporary Sociology*, 39: 530–532.

Braithwaite, J. (2011). "Opportunities and Dangers of Capitalist Criminology." In S. Parmentier, L. Walgrave, I. Aertsen, J. Maesschalck, and L. Paoli (Eds.) *The Sparking Discipline of Criminology*. Leuven, Belgium: Leuven University Press.

Bretton Woods Project (2006). "The World Bank Weeds Out Corruption: Will It Touch the Roots?" *Update 50*. Available online from: <http://www.brettonwoodsproject.org/art-531789> (Accessed February 23, 2013).

Bretton Woods Project (2012). "The World Bank and Extractives: A Rich Seam of Controversy." Available online from: <http://www.brettonwoodsproject.org/art-569560> (Accessed September 3, 2013).

Bretton Woods Project (2013). "The Founding Fathers." Available online from: <http://external.worldbankimflib.org/Bwf/60panel3.htm> (Accessed September 12, 2013).

Broad, R. (Ed.) (2002). *Global Backlash: Citizen Initiatives for a Just World Economy*. Lanham, MD: Rowman and Littlefield.

Cain, M. (2010). "Crimes of the Global State." In F. Brookman, M. Maguire, H. Pierpoint, and T. Bennett. *Handbook on Crime* (pp. 801–824), Cullompton/Portland, OR: Willan.

Cardhoff, S. (2011). "Newmont Planning to Advance Akyem Mine Project in Ghana Forest Reserve." Available online from: <http://www.earthworksaction.org/earthblog/detail/newmont_planning_to_advane_akyem_mine_project_in_ghana_forest_reserve#.UcSvN_XD9D8> (Accessed September 4, 2013).

Castells, M. (2004). *The Information Age: Economy, Society, and Culture*. Cambridge, MA: Blackwell.

Center for Science and Public Participation. (2005). Environmental Impact Assessment. *Technical Review Environmental and Social Impact Assessment AHAFO SOUTH PROJECT*. Available online from: <http://www.csp2.org/files/reports/CSP2_Comments_Ahafo_South_12_05.pdf> (Accessed October 9, 2013).

Chambliss, W. J. (1989). "State-Organized Crime—The American Society of Criminology, 1988 Presidential Address." *Criminology*, 27(2): 183–207.

Chan, S. (2010). "Poorer Nations Get Larger Role in World Bank." *New York Times* (April 26): B3.

Cohen, L. E. and M. Felson. (1979). "Social Change and Crime Rate Trends: A Routine Activity Approach." *American Sociological Review*, 44: 588–605.

Cohen, S. (1988). *Against Criminology*. New Brunswick, Canada: Transaction Books.

Coleman, R., Sim, J., Tombs, S., and Whyte, D. (Eds.) (2009). *State, Power, Crime*. Los Angeles, CA: Sage.

Common Dreams (2012). "Group to World Bank: Stop Funding Water Privatization." Available online from: <https://www.commondreams.org/headline/2012/04/16-2> (Accessed September 4, 2013).

Compliance Advisor Ombudsman (CAO) (2012). "Annual Report 2012." Available online from: <http://www.caoombudsman.org/documents/CAOAnnualReport2012.pdf> (Accessed September 3, 2013).

Cornish, D. B. and Clarke, R. V. (Eds.) (1986). *The Reasoning Criminal: Rational Choice Perspectives on Offending*. New York: Springer-Verlag.

Corporate Accountability International (2012). "Shutting the Spigot on Private Water: The Case for the World Bank to Divest." Available online from: <http://www.stopcorporateabuse.org/sites/default/files/resources/shutting_the_spigot_on_private_water_corporateaccountabilityinternational.pdf> (Accessed September 4, 2013).

Croall, H. (2005). "Transnational White-Collar Crime." In J. Sheptycki and A. Wardak (Eds.) *Transnational and Comparative Criminology*. London: Glasshouse Press.

Cullen, F. T. and Agnew, R. (2003). *Criminological Theory: Past to Present*. Los Angeles, CA: Roxbury Park.

Dadush, U. and Dervis, K. (2013). "The Inequality Challenge." *Current History* (January): 13–19.

Darian-Smith, E. (Ed.) (2013). *Law and Societies in Global Contexts*. New York: Cambridge University Press.

Dauagirdas, K. (2013). "Congress Underestimated: The Case of the World Bank." *American Journal of International Law* 107 (July): 517–562.

Dean, P. and Ritzer, G. (2012). "Globalization." In G. Ritzer (Ed.) *The Wiley-Blackwell Companion to Sociology*. Malden, MA: Wiley-Blackwell.

DeKeseredy, W. and Dragiewicz, M. (Eds.) (2012). *Routledge Handbook of Critical Criminology*. New York: Routledge.

Doctorow, E. L. (2008). "The White Whale." *The Nation*, July 14: 28–32.

Dunai, M. and Szakacs, G. (2013). "Hungary Repays 2008 IMF Loan in Full-Government." Available online from: <http://uk.reuters.com/article/2013/08/12/uk-hungary-imf-repaid-idUKBRE97B07720130812> (Accessed September 4, 2013).

Durkheim, É. (1897). *Le Suicide: étude de sociologie*. Paris: Alcan.

Ellwood, W. (2010). *The No-Nonsense Guide to Globalization*. Oxford: New Internationalist.

Erlichman, H. J. (2010). *Conquest, Tribute, and Trade: The Quest for Precious Metals and the Birth of Globalization*. New York: Prometheus Press.

Ersado, L. (2012). "Income Inequality and Inequality of Opportunity: Cues from Egypt's Arab Spring." Available online from: <http://menablog. worldbank.org/income-inequality-and-inequality-opportunity-cues-egypt%E2%80%99s-arab-spring> (Accessed September 5, 2013).

Escobar, A. (2000). "Notes on Networks and Anti-Globalization Social Movements." Paper Presented at the Annual American Anthropological Association Meeting, University of North Carolina, Chapel Hill, November.

European Union (1997). Convention against Corruption Involving Officials. *Official Journal* C-195 (25 June 1997).

European Union (1999). Civil Law Convention on Corruption. Available online from: <http://conventions.coe.int/Treaty/en/Treaties/Html/174. htm> (Accessed March 12, 2014).

European Union (2007). Convention on the Protection of the European Communities Financial Interests. P6_TA (2007)0441.

Ewald, U. (2008). "Reason and Truth in International Criminal Justice: A Criminological Perspective on the Construction of Evidence in International Trials." In Smeulers, A. and Haveman R. (Eds.) *Supranational Criminology: Towards a Criminology of International Crimes* (pp. 399–432), Antwerp: Intersentia.

Extractive Industries Source Book. (2013). "Good-Fit Practice Activities in the International Oil, Gas, and Mining Industries." Available online from: <http://www.eisourcebook.org/> (Accessed September 3, 2013).

Extractive Industries Transparency Initiative. (2013). "Countries Included in the World Bank Extraction Industry Transparency Initiative Reports" Available online from: <http://www.eisourcebook.org/> (Accessed September 3, 2013).

Ezeonu, I. (2008). "Crimes of Globalization: Health Care, HIV and the Poverty of Neo-Liberalism in Sub-Saharan Africa." *International Journal of Social Inquiry*, 113–134.

Ezeonu, I. and Koku, E. (2008). "Crimes of Globalization: The Feminization of HIV Pandemic in Sub-Saharan Africa." *The Global South*, 2(2): 112–129.

Farnworth, M. (1989). "Theory Integration versus Model Building." In *Theoretical Integration in the Study of Crime and Delinquency: Problems and Prospects* (pp. 93–100), Albany, NY: State University of New York Press.

Ferguson, N. (2005). *Colossus: The Rise and Fall of the American Empire*. New York: Penguin Books.

Findlay, M. (1999). *The Globalization of Crime: Understanding Transitional Relationships in Context*. Cambridge: Cambridge University Press.

Findlay, M. and Henham, R. (2005). *Transforming International Criminal Justice: Retributive and Restorative Justice in the Trial Process*. Cullompton: Willan.

Fischman, J. (2011). "Criminal minds." *Chronicle Review* (June 17): B6–B8.

Fiss, P. C., and Hirsch, P. M. (2005). "The Discourse of Globalization: Framing and Sensemaking of an Emerging Concept." *American Sociological Review*, 70: 29–52.

Foucault, M. (1977). *Discipline and Punish: The Birth of the Prison*. Alan Sheridan (trans.), New York: Vintage.

Foucault, M. (1980). "Truth and Power." In *Power/Knowledge: Selected Interview Writings, 1972–1977* (pp. 109–133), New York: Pantheon Books.

Freeman, L. (2004). *The Development of Social Network Analysis: A Study in the Sociology of Science*. Vancouver, Canada: Empirical Press.

Friedman, T. (2005). *The World Is Flat: A Brief History of the Twenty-first Century*. New York: Farrar, Straus, and Giroux.

Friedrichs, D. O. (1992). "White Collar Crime and the Definitional Quagmire: A Provisional Solution." *Journal of Human Justice*, 3: 5–21.

Friedrichs, D. O. (2007). "White-collar Crime in a Postmodern, Globalized World." In H. N. Pontell and G. Geis (Eds.) *International Handbook of White-Collar and Corporate Crime* (pp. 163–184), New York: Springer.

Friedrichs, D. O. (2010). *Trusted Criminals: White Collar Crime in Contemporary Society*, 4th ed. Stamford, CT: Cengage Learning.

Friedrichs, D. O., and Friedrichs, J. (2002). "The World Bank and Crimes of Globalization: A Case Study." *Social Justice*, 29(1–2): 1–12.

Friedrichs, D. O., and Rothe, D. L. (2013). "Crimes of Globalization as a Criminological Project: The Case of International Financial Institutions." In F. Pakes (Ed.) *Globalisation and the Challenge to Criminology* (pp. 45–63), New York: Routledge.

Friedrichs, D. O. and Rothe, D. L. (forthcoming) "State-Corporate Crime and Major Financial Institutions: Interrogating an Absence." *State Crime*.

Friedrichs, D. O., and Schwartz, M. D. (2007). "Editors' Introduction: On Social Harm and a Twenty-First Century Criminology." *Crime, Law and Social Change*, 48: 1–7.

Friman, H. R. (Ed.) (2009). *Crime and the Global Political Economy*. Boulder, CO: Lynne Rienner Publishers.

Garton, J. (2009). *The Regulation of Organised Society*. Oxford: Hart Publishing.

Ghemawat, P. (2007). "Why the World Isn't Flat." *Foreign Policy*, (March–April): 54–60.

Gibbons, D. C. (1979). *The Criminological Enterprise: Theories and Perspectives*. Englewood Cliffs, NJ: Prentice-Hall, Inc.

Goldman, M. (2005). *Imperial Nature: The World Bank and Struggles for Justice in the Age of Globalization.* New Haven, CT: Yale University Press.

Gorchinskava, K. (2013). "Azarov: Ukraine Ready to Borrow Internationally, Not Ready to Concede to IMF Demands." Available online from: <http://www.kyivpost.com/content/ukraine/azarov-ukraine-ready-to-borrow-internationally-not-ready-to-concede-to-imf-demands-319039.html> (Accessed September 3, 2013).

Grabosky, P. (2009). "Globalization and White-Collar Crime." In S. S. Simpson and D. Weisburd (Eds.) *The Criminology of White Collar Crime.* New York: Springer.

Graeber, D. (2011). *Debt: The First 5,000 Years.* Brooklyn, NY: Melville House.

Green, P. and Ward, T. (2004). *State Crime: Governments, Violence and Corruption.* London: Pluto.

Greste, P. (2009). "The Dam that Divides Ethiopians." Available online from: <http://news.bbc.co.uk/2/hi/africa/7959444.stm> (Accessed September 4, 2013).

Guay, J. (2013). "Kosovo Activists Project No Coal on World Bank Building." Available online from: <http://www.huffingtonpost.com/justin-guay/kosovo-activists-project-_b_3022690.html> (Accessed September 4, 2013).

Hagan, J. and Rymond-Richmond, W. (2009). *Darfur and the Crime of Genocide.* New York: Cambridge University Press.

Hauhart, R. C. (2012). "Toward a Sociology of Criminological Theory." *The American Sociologist,* 43, 153–171.

Hawley, S. (2000). "Exporting Corruption, Privatization, Multinationals and Bribery." Available online from: <http://www.thecornerhouse.org.uk/item.shtml?x=51975> (Accessed June 21, 2009).

Held, D. (Ed.) (2005). *Debating Globalization.* Malden, MA: Polity Press.

Henry, S. and Lanier, M. M. (2001). *What Is Crime? Controversies over the Nature of Crime and What to Do about It.* Lanham, MD: Rowman and Littlefield Publishers.

Hiatt, S. (2007). *A Game as Old as Empire: The Secret World of Economic Hit Men and the Web of Global Corruption.* San Francisco, CA: Berrett-Koehler Inc.

Hillyard, P., Pantazis, C., Tombs, S., and Gordon, D. (Eds.) (2004). *Beyond Criminology: Taking Harm Seriously.* London: Pluto Press.

Hubbard, B., Kirkpatrick, D. D., and El Sheikh, M. (2013). "Morsi Supporters Face Crackdown, Deepening Divide." *New York Times,* (July 5): A1.

Human Rights Watch (2012a). "Ethiopia, Kenya: World Bank Approves Controversial Loan: Decision Ignores Gibe III Dam's Impact on Indigenous

Peoples, Environmental Concerns." Available online from: <http://www.hrw.org/news/2012/07/13/ethiopia-kenya-world-bank-approves-controversial-loan> (Accessed September 4, 2013).

Human Rights Watch (2012b). "Waiting Here for Death: Forced Displacement and 'Villagization' in Ethiopia's Gambella Region." Available online from: <http://www.hrw.org/sites/default/files/reports/ethiopia0112webwcover_0.pdf> (Accessed September 4, 2013).

Human Rights Watch (2013). "Abuse-Free Development: How the World Bank Should Safeguard Against Human Rights Violations." Available online from: <http://www.hrw.org/node/117248> (Accessed September 4, 2013).

Hyman, L. (2011). *Debtor Nation: The History of America in Red Ink*. Princeton, NJ: Princeton University Press.

Independent Evaluation Office of the International Monetary Fund (2012) "International Reserves: IMF Concerns and Country Perspectives." Available online from: <http://www.ieo-imf.org/ieo/files/completedevaluations/IR_Main_Report.pdf> (Accessed November 3, 2014).

International Finance Corporation (2011). "IFC Makes Its First Investment in Côte d'Ivoire's Mining Sector through Sama Resources." Available online from: <http://ifcext.ifc.org/IFCExt/Pressroom/IFCPressRoom.nsf/0/BFECBE778C94C6C98525796C005BFC00> (Accessed September 12, 2013).

International Finance Corporation (2013 appendix). "Projects: Summary of Investment Information." Available online from: <http://www.ifc.org/wps/wcm/connect/Industry_EXT_Content/IFC_External_Corporate_Site/Industries/Infrastructure/Sectors/WaterAndUtilities/> (Accessed September 12, 2013).

International Finance Corporation (2013a). "IFC Global Mining." Available online from: <http://www.ifc.org/wps/wcm/connect/434c0a0049a5f8cda3d0e3a8c6a8312a/IFC+Mining+Overview.pdf?MOD=AJPERES> (Accessed September 4, 2013).

International Finance Corporation (2013b). "Water and Utilities." Available online from: <http://www.ifc.org/wps/wcm/connect/industry_ext_content/ifc_external_corporate_site/industries/infrastructure/sectors/waterandutilities> (Accessed September 4, 2013).

International Monetary Fund (2013a). "About the IMF." Available online from: <http://www.imf.org/external/about.htm> (Accessed September 4, 2013).

International Monetary Fund (2013b). "Overview." Available online from: <http://www.imf.org/external/about/overview.htm> (Accessed February 1, 2013).

International Rivers (2011). "Ethiopia's Gibe III Dam: Sowing Hunger and Conflict." Available online from: < http://www.internationalrivers.org/files/attached- files/gibe3factsheet2011.pdf> (Accessed September 4, 2013).

International Rivers (2012). "Gibe III Dam, Ethiopia." Available online from: <http://www.internationalrivers.org/campaigns/gibe-iii-dam-ethiopia> (Accessed September 4, 2013).

Jackson, R. (2012). *Occupy World Street: A Global Roadmap for Radical Economic and Political Reform*. White River Junction, VT: Chelsea Green Publishing.

Kaja, A. and Werker, E. (2009). "Corporate Misgovernance at the World Bank." Working paper 09-108, Harvard Business School. Available online from: <http://www.hbs.edu/faculty/Publication%20Files/09-108.pdf> (Accessed September 13, 2013).

Kaldor, M., Moore, L., and Selchow, S. (2012). *Global Civil Society, 2012: Ten Years of Reflection*. New York: Palgrave Macmillan.

Kalleberg, R. (2005). "What is 'Public Sociology'? Why and How It Should Be Made Stronger." *British Journal of Sociology*, 56: 387–393.

Kanowicz, S. (2010). "The United States Exploits Borrowing by Developing Countries." In C. Fisanick (Ed.) *Debt*. Detroit, MI: Gale/Cengage.

Kant. I. (1795). Perpetual Peace Online. Available online from: <http://www.mtholyoke.edu/acad/intrel/kant/kant1.htm> or <http://perpetualpeace-project.org/resources/kant.php> (Accessed November 3, 2014).

Karstedt, S. and Nelken, D. (Eds.) (2013). *Crime and Globalization*. Surrey: Ashgate.

Kauzlarich, D. and Kramer, R. (1998). *Crimes of the American Nuclear State: At Home and Abroad*. Boston, MA: Northeastern University Press.

Kenny, C. (2011). "Attention Doomsayers: Global Quality of Life Is Improving." *Chronicle Review*, (April 1): B10–11.

Khagram, R. (2006). "Possible Future Architectures of Global Governance: A Transnational Perspective/Prospective." *Global Governance*, 12: 97–117.

Knepper, P. (2012). "Measuring the Threat of Global Crime: Insights from Research by the League of Nations into the Traffic of Women." *Criminology*, 50: 777–809.

Kramer, R. and Michalowski, R. (1990). *Toward an Integrated Theory of State-Corporate Crime*. Presented at the American Society of Criminology, Baltimore, MD.

Kurlantzick, J. (2008). "The World is Bumpy." *The New Republic* (July 15): 19–21.

Kuttner, R. (2013). "The Debt We Shouldn't Pay." *The New York Review of Books* (May 9): 16–18.

Kyte, R. (2011). "Mining, Oil and Gas Riches: From Elite Plunder to Development Promise." *World Bank*. Available online from: <http://web.worldbank.org/WBSITE/EXTERNAL/TOPICS/EXTSDNET/0,,contentMDK:23082124~menuPK:64885113~pagePK:7278667~piPK:64911824~theSitePK:5929282,00.html> (Accessed September 3, 2013).

Langman, L. and Morris, D. (2012). "Internet Mediation: A Theory of Alternative Movements." In M. Gurstein and S. Finquelievich (Eds.) *Proceedings of the 1st International Workshop on Community Informatics.* Montreal, Canada. Available online from: <http://www.csudh.edu/dearharbermas/langmanbk01.htm> (Accessed October 8, 2013).

Larsen, N. and Smandych, R. (Eds.) (2008). *Global Criminology and Criminal Justice: Current Issues and Perspectives.* Peterborough, Ontario, Canada: Broadview Press.

Liska, A., Krohn, M. and Messner, S. (1989). "Strategies and Requisites for Theoretical Integration in the Study of Crime and Deviance." In *Theoretical Integration in the Study of Crime and Delinquency: Problems and Prospects* (pp. 1–20), Albany, NY: State University of New York Press.

Loader, I. and Sparks, R. (2011). *Public Criminology?* London: Routledge.

Mackenzie, S. (2006). "Systematic Crimes of the Powerful: Criminal Aspects of the Global Economy." *Social Justice*, 33(1): 162–182.

Madrick, J. (2013). "The Anti-Economist." *Harper's Magazine*, (August): 9–11.

Mainhardt, H. and Sinani, N. (2013). "World Bank Kosovo Power Project Environmental and Social Impact Assessment: Comment on the Kosovo lber Lepenc Water System Study." Available online from: <http://www.bicusa.org/wp-content/uploads/2013/01/Kosovo+Water+Study.pdf> (Accessed September 4, 2013).

Marfleet, P. (2013). "Mubarak's Egypt – Nexus of Criminality." *State Crime* 2, (Autumn): 112–135.

Mason, P. (2012). *Why It's Kicking Off Everywhere: The New Global Revolutions.* London: Verso.

Merton, R. K. (1938). "Social Structure and Anomie." *American Sociological Review*, 3: 672–682.

Michalowski, R. J. and Kramer, R. (Eds.) (2006). *State-Corporate Crime: Wrongdoing at the Intersection of Business and Government.* Piscataway, NY: Rutgers University Press.

Michalowski, R. and Kramer, R. (2014). "Transnational Environmental Crime." In P. Reichel and J. Albanese (Eds.) *Handbook of Transnational Crime and Justice*, 2nd ed., Los Angeles, CA: Sage.

Monaghan, P. (2009). "Biocriminology." *Chronicle of Higher Education*, (April 17): B4–B5.

Moody, J. and White, D. (2003). "Structural Cohesion and Embeddedness: A Hierarchical Concept of Social Groups." *American Sociological Review*, 68: 103–127.

Murphy, T. and Whitty, N. (2013). "Making History: Academic Criminology and Human Rights." *British Journal of Criminology*, 53: 568–587.

Mychalejko, C. (2005). "World Bank Mining Project in Guatemala: Glamis Gold Gets $45 Million to Construct a Mine." *Third World Traveler*. Available online from: <http://www.thirdworldtraveler.com/Central_America/WB_Mining_Guatemala.html> (Accessed September 4, 2013).

Myren, R. (1980) "Justiciology: An Idea Whose Time Has Come." *The Justice Reporter* 1: 1–7.

Nelken, D. (Ed.) (1994). *The Futures of Criminology*. London: Sage.

Nelken, D. (Ed.) (2011). *Comparative Criminal Justice and Globalization*. Surrey: Ashgate Publishing.

Newmont. (2011). "The Socio-Economic Impact of Newmont Ghana Gold Limited" Available online from: <http://www.newmont.com/sites/default/files/Socio_Economic_Impact_of_Newmont_Ghana_Gold_July_2011_0_0.pdf> (Accessed September 4, 2013).

Newmont. (2013). "Beyond the Mine: The Journey towards Sustainability: Africa." Available online from: <http://www.beyondthemine.com/2012/about_newmont/newmont_operations_map/africa> (Accessed September 4, 2013).

No Dirty Gold. (2010). *Ahafo Mine*. Available online from: <http://www.nodirtygold.org/wassa_district_ghana.cfm> (Accessed September 12, 2013).

Nollkaemper, A. (2009). "Introduction." In *System Criminality in International Law* (pp. 1–26), Cambridge: Cambridge University Press.

Nollkaemper, A. and Van der Wilt, H. (Eds.) (2009). *System Criminality in International Law* (pp. 1–26), Cambridge: Cambridge University Press.

North, J. (2011). "The Roots of the Cote d'Ivoire Crisis." *The Nation*, (April 25): 24–26.

Oatley, T. (2009). *International Political Economy*, 4th ed., London: Longman.

Organization for Economic Corporation and Development (OECD) (1997). Convention on Combating Bribery of Foreign Public Officials in International Business Transactions. Available online from: <http://www.oecd.org/corruption/oecdantibriberyconvention.htm> (Accessed March 12, 2014).

Owusu-Koranteng, D. (2010). "15 Killed in Course of Newmont Ahafo Mine Operations." Available online from: <http://ghanaweb.com/mobile/wap.small/news.article.php?ID=197006> (Accessed September 4, 2013).

Pakes, F. (Ed.) (2013). *Globalisation and the Challenge to Criminology*. New York: Routledge.

Parmentier, S., Walgrave, L., Aertsen, I., Maesschalck, J., and Paoli, L. (Eds.) (2011). *The Sparking Discipline of Criminology: John Braithwaite and the Construction of Critical Social Science and Social Justice*. Leuven, Belgium: Leuven University Press.

Perkins, J. (2005). *Confessions of an Economic Hit Man*. New York: Plume Books.

Perkins, J. (2007). *The Secret History of the American Empire: The Truth about Economic Hit Men, Jackals, and How to Change the World*. New York: Plume Books.

Pleyers, G. (2011). *Alter-Globalization: Becoming Actors in the Global Age*. Malden, MA: Polity.

Popper, K. (1959). *The Logic of Scientific Discovery*. London: Routledge.

Prashad, V. (2012). *The Poorer Nations: A Possible History of the Global South*. London: Verso.

Rafter, N. (2004a). "Earnest A. Hooton and the Biological Tradition in American Criminology." *Criminology*, 42: 735–771.

Rafter, N. (2004b). "The Unrepentant Horse-Slasher: Moral Insanity and the Origins of Criminological Thought." *Criminology*, 42: 979–1008.

Raine, A. (2013). *The Anatomy of Violence*. New York: Pantheon.

Rastogi, N. S. (2010). "Production of Gold has Many Negative Environmental Effects." *Huffington Post*. (September 21). Available online from: <http://www.washingtonpost.com/wp-dyn/content/article/2010/09/20/AR2010092004730.html> (Accessed September 4, 2013).

Reichel, P. and Albanese, J. (2014). *Handbook of Transnational Crime and Justice*, 2nd ed., Thousand Oaks, CA: Sage.

Robinson, M. (2004). *Why Crime? An Integrated Systems Theory of Antisocial Behavior*. Upper Saddle River, NJ: Pearson.

Rosenfeld, R (2002). "Book Review of Crime: Public Policies for Crime Control." Available online from: <http://www.thefreelibrary.com/Crime%3A+Public+Policies+for+Crime+Controla0105440476> (Accessed February 20, 2013).

Rothe, D. L. (2006). *The Masquerade of Abu Ghraib: State Crime, Torture, and International Law*. Dissertation. On file at Western Michigan University.

Rothe, D. L. (2009). *State Criminality: The Crime of All Crimes*. Lanham, Maryland: Lexington/Roman and Littlefield.

Rothe, D. L. (2010a). "International Financial Institutions, Corruption and Human Rights." In Martine Boersma and Hans Nelen (Eds.) *Corruption and Human Rights* (pp. 177–197), Antwerp: Intersentia.

Rothe, D. L. (2010b). "Facilitating Corruption and Human Rights Violations: The Role of International Financial Institutions." *Crime, Law and Social Change*, 53(5): 457–476.

Rothe, D. L. and Collins, V. (2011). "An Exploration of System Criminality and Arms Trafficking." *International Criminal Justice Review*, 21(1): 22–38.

Rothe, D. L. and Friedrichs, D. (2013). "Controlling Crimes of Globalization: A Challenge for International Criminal Justice" In W. de Lint, M. Marmo, and N. Chazal (Eds.). *Crime and Justice in International Society*. New York: Routledge.

Rothe, D. L. and Mullins, C. (2008). "Genocide, War Crimes and Crimes against Humanity in Central Africa: A Criminological Exploration." In *Supranational Criminology: Towards a Criminology of International Crimes* (pp. 135–158), Antwerp: Intersentia.

Rothe, D. L., Mullins, C. W., and Muzzatti, S. (2006). "Crime on the High Seas: Crimes of Globalization and the Sinking of the Senegalese Ferry Le Joola." *Critical Criminology: An International Journal*, 14(2): 159–180.

Rothe, D. L., Mullins, C. W., and Sandstrom, K. (2009). "The Rawandan Genocide: International Finance Policies and Human Rights." *Social Justice*, 35(3): 66–86.

Rothe, D. L. and Ross, J. I. (2010). "Private Military Contractors, Crime, and the Terrain of Unaccountability." *Justice Quarterly*, 27(4): 593–617.

Roundtree, P., Land, W. and Miethe, T. D. (1994). "Macro-Micro Integration in the Study of Victimization: A Hierarchical Logistic Model Analysis across Seattle Neighborhood." *Criminology*, 32(3): 387–414.

Samar, V. J. (2011). "A Preface to World Government." *Connecticut Journal of International Law*, 27: 1–37.

Sarfaty, G. A. (2012). *Values in Translation: Human Rights and the Culture of the World Bank*. Stanford: Stanford University Press.

Saul, J. R. (2005). *The Collapse of Globalism and the Reinvention of the World*. New York: Penguin.

Savelsberg, J. (2010). *Crime and Human Rights: Criminology of Genocide and Atrocities*. Los Angeles, CA: Sage.

Savelsberg, J. J., and Flood, S. M. (2004). "Criminological Knowledge: Period and Cohort Effects in Scholarship." *Criminology*, 43: 327–348.

Sawyer, S. and Gomez, E. T. (2008). "Transnational Governmentality and Resource Extraction: Indigenous Peoples, Multinational Corporations, Multilateral Institutions and the State." *Identities, Conflict and Cohesion Programme Paper Number 13*. (September 2008).

Schneider, H. (2012). "Auditor Finds IMF Was Pressured By U.S. to Fault China." *The Washington Post, Home Collections*. Available online from: <http://articles.washingtonpost.com/2012-12-19/business/35929398_1_foreign-reserves-imf-staff-ieo> (Accessed February 13, 2013).

Schwendinger, H. and Schwendinger, J. (1970). "Defenders of Order or Guardians of Human Rights?' *Issues in Criminology*, 5: 123–157.

Shah, A. (2008). "Corruption." *Global Issues*. Available online from: <http://www.globalissues.org/article/590/corruption#> (Accessed June 26. 2009).

Shaman, D. (2009). *The World Bank Unveiled: Inside the Revolutionary Struggle for Transparency*. Little Rock, AR: Parkhurst Brothers.

Shelley, L. (2011). "The Globalization of Crime." In M. Natarajan (Ed.) *International Crime and Justice*. New York: Cambridge University Press.

Sheptycki, J. and Wardak, A. (Eds.) (2005). *Transnational and Comparative Criminology*. London: Glasshouse Press.

Skidelsky, R. (2008). "Gloomy about Globalization." *New York Review of Books*, (April 17): 60–64.

Slade, J. W. (2000). *Pornography in America: A Reference Handbook*. Santa Barbara, CA: ABC-CLIO.

Smith, K. E. I. (Ed.) (2013). *Sociology of Globalization*. Boulder, CO: Westview Press.

Spier, F. (2010). *Big History and the Future of Humanity*. Malden, MA: Wiley-Blackwell.

Stanley, E. (2009). *Torture, Truth and Justice: The Case of Timor-Leste*. Abingdon: Routledge.

Stiglitz, J. (2002). *Globalization and Its Discontents*. New York: Norton and Company.

Stiglitz, J. (2006). *Making Globalization Work*. New York: W. W. Norton.

Strom, S. (2011). "Cracking Open the World Bank." *New York Times*, (July 3): Bus.1.

Stroup, S. S. (2012). *Borders among Activists: International NGOs in the United States, Britain, and France*. Ithaca, NY: Cornell University Press.

Sutherland, E. H. (1940). "White-Collar Criminality." *American Sociological Review*, 5: 1–12.

Sutherland, E. H. (1945). "Is 'White-Collar Crime' Crime?" *American Sociological Review*, 12: 132–139.

Sutherland, E. (1949). *White Collar Crime*. New York: Holt, Rinehart and Winston.

Sykes, G. and Matza, D. (1957). "Techniques of Neutralization: A Theory of Delinquency." *American Sociological Review*, 22: 664–70.

Tappan, P. (1947). "Who Is the Criminal?" *American Sociological Review*, 12: 96–102.

The Inter-American Convention Against Corruption (1996). Published by the Organization of American States. Available online from: <http://www.oas.org/juridico/english/corr_bg.htm> (Accessed March 13, 2014).

The New Indian Express (2013). "World Bank Team Faces Protests." (April 2013). Available online from: <http://newindianexpress.com/states/odisha/World-Bank-team-faces-protests/2013/04/11/article1539813.ece> (Accessed June, 3 2012).

The World Bank (2012). "Global Development Finance: External Debt of Developing Countries." Available online from: <http://data.worldbank.org/sites/default/files/gdf_2012.pdf> (Accessed September 5, 2013).

Tifft, L. L. and Sullivan, D. C. (1980). *The Struggle to Be Human: Crime, Criminology and Anarchism*. Sanday, Orkney: Cienfuegoes Press.

Tombs, S. and Whyte, D. (2007). *Safety Crimes*. Portland, OR: Willan.

Torrance, M. and Lochery, E. (2008). *An analysis of the IFIs' Fiscal Policy Recommendations*. The Oxford Council on Good Governance. Available online from: <http://ocgg.org/fileadmin/Publications/EY008.pdf.> (Accessed June 27, 2009).

Toussaint, E. (2005). "Regulating the Public and the Private Economy: The IMF, the World Bank, and Respect of Human Rights." Available online from: <http://www.world-governance.org/spip.php?article43> (Accessed October 11, 2013).

Toussaint, E. and Millet, D. (2010). *Debt, the IMF, and the World Bank: Sixty Questions, Sixty Anwers*. New York: Monthly Review Press.

Underhill, G. (2000). "State, Market, and Global Political Economy: Genealogy of an (Inter-?) Discipline." *International Affairs*, 76: 805–824. United Nations General Assembly (UNGA) (1974). *Declaration on the Establishment of a New International Economic Order*. A/RES/S-6/3201.

United Nations General Assembly (UNGA) (2003). Convention on Economic, Social and Cultural Human Rights. Available online from: <http://www.ohchr.org/EN/ProfessionalInterest/Pages/CESCR.aspx> (Accessed March 12, 2014).

United Nations General Assembly (UNGA) (2011). *The Guiding Principles on Business and Human Rights: Implementing the United Nations "Protect, Respect and Remedy" Framework*. A/HRC/17/31.

United Nations Office on Drugs and Crime. (2004a). *Convention against Corruption*. General Assembly Resolution 58/4 (31 October 2003).

United Nations Office on Drugs and Crime (2004b) *Convention against Transnational Organized Crime*. Available online from: <http://www.unodc.org/documents/treaties/UNTOC/Publications/TOC%20Convention/TOCebook-e.pdf.> (Accessed March 13, 2014).

United Nations Sub-Commission on the Promotion and Protection of Human Rights (2003). *Norms on the Responsibilities of Transnational Corporations and Other Business Enterprises with Regard to Human Rights Agreement*. UN Document E/CN.4/Sub.2/2003/38/Rev.2 (26 August 2003).

Universal Declaration of Human Rights (1948). Published by the United Nations General Assembly. Available online from: <http://www.ohchr.org/en/udhr/pages/introduction.aspx> (Accessed March 13, 2014).

Van Boven, T. C., Flinterman, C., and Westendorp, I. (1997). *The Maastricht Guidelines on Violations of Economic, Social and Cultural Rights*. SIM: Special No. 2.

Vaughan, D. (1982). "Toward Understanding Unlawful Organizational Behavior." *Michigan Law Review*, 80: 1377–1402.

Vaughan, D. (2002). "Criminology and the Sociology of Organizations." *Crime, Law and Social Change,* 37(2): 117–136.

Vico, G. (1948). *The New Science of Giambattista Vico*, T. G. Bergin and M. H. Fisch (trans.), Ithaca, NY: Cornell University Press.

von Bulow, M. (2010). *Building Transnational Networks: Civil Society and the Politics of Trade in the Americas*. New York: Cambridge University Press.

Walgrave, L. (2011). "Between Evangelism and Charlatanism. Reflections on the Social Responsibility of Criminology and Other Social Sciences." In S. Parmentier, L.Walgrave, I. Aersen, J. Maesschalck, and L. Paoli (Eds.). *The Sparking Discipline of Criminology*, (pp. 11–32), Leuven: Leuven University Press.

Watts, R., Bessant, J., and Hil, R. (2008). *International Criminology: A Critical Introduction*. London: Routledge.

Weaver, C. (2008). *Hypocrisy Trap: The World Bank and the Poverty of Reform*. Ithaca, NY: Cornell University Press.

Welch, M. (2008). "Foucault in a Post-9/11 World: Excursions into Security, Territory, Population." In *Discipline, Security, and Beyond: Rethinking Michael Foucault*. College of France de'Lectures. Carcel Notebooks. Available online from: <http://www.thecarceral.org/cn4_welch.pdf > (Accessed February 20, 2013).

Wellford, C. F. (1989). "Towards an Integrated Theory of Criminal Behavior." In *Theoretical Integration in the Study of Deviance and Crime: Problems and Prospects*, (pp. 119–128). Albany, NY: State University of New York Press.

Wetzell, R. F. (2000). *Inventing the Criminal: A History of German Criminology*. Chapel Hill, NC: University of North Carolina Press.

Woods, N. (2006). Quoted in Guttall, S. (2006). "Fuelling Discontent: The World Bank and International Monetary Fund in Singapore." (p. 5). Available online from: <http://alainet.org/active/13945> (Accessed May 1, 2009).

World Development Movement (2013). "Destructive World Bank Projects Around the World." Available online from: <http://www.wdm.org.uk/our-campaignclimate-justice/destructive-world-bank-projects-around-world> (Accessed September 4, 2013).

Wright, W. and Muzzatti, S. (2007). "Not in My Port: The 'Death Ship' of Sheep and Crimes of Agri-Food Globalization." *Agriculture and Human Values*, 24: 133–145.

Young, J. (2011). *The Criminological Imagination*. Cambridge: Polity Press.

Zumbasen, P. (2012). "Defining the Space of Transnational Law: Legal Theory, Global Governance, and Legal Pluralism." *Transnational Law and Contemporary Problems*, 21: 305–335.

Zweifel, T. D. (2006). *International Organizations and Democracy: Accountability, Politics, and Power*. Boulder, CO: Lynne Rienner.

INDEX